FIRST WORLD WAR
IN THE AIR

D0885799

FIRST WORLD WAR
IN THE AIR

PHIL CARRADICE

AMBERLEY

First published 2012

Amberley Publishing
The Hill, Stroud
Gloucestershire, GL5 4EP
www.amberleybooks.com

British Library Cataloguing in Publication Data.
A catalogue record for this book is available from the British Library.

ISBN 978 1 4456 0512 8

Typeset in 10pt on 13pt Sabon LT.
Typesetting and Origination by Amberley Publishing.
Printed in the UK.

CONTENTS

ACKNOWLEDGEMENTS

First and foremost thanks are due to my late father and grandfather who, fascinated by the aerial war of 1914 to 1918, passed on their enthusiasm to me. One of my treasured possessions is a copy of *Winged Victory*, given to me by my father at Christmas 1961 when the Great War was still a living memory to many people. It is one of my deepest regrets that neither my father nor my grandfather is alive now to enjoy – and undoubtedly criticise – this book.

Thanks are due to the secretaries and friends of numerous cemeteries across Britain, all of whom willingly sent me lists of RFC and RAF airmen who had died in the war and were buried in British graveyards – as opposed to the war cemeteries in France and Belgium. It was not possible to include references or names but the information was invaluable in creating background knowledge.

A huge thank you has to go to Paul Kemp of Barry who owns and runs the Paul Kemp Archive. He willingly allowed me to quote from diaries and MSS in the collection, first hand and primary source material that has given this book more credibility than it might otherwise have deserved and enjoyed.

Most of the photographs used in this book are from my own collection. However, thanks are due to the following, either for use of images or for advice and help with reproductions:

Roger McCallum
Trudy Carradice
The Keasbury-Gordon Archive

As ever, huge thanks to Trudy, my wife, who supported, criticised and advised – all at appropriate moments.

INTRODUCTION

This book is an attempt to tell the story of the conflict in the air during the four years of the Great War. It could never hope to be a full history, recounting every incident, every drama, every heroic event and death that ever occurred. Rather, it tries to provide a general sweep, facts and photographs blending together to create an interesting but informative narrative. The word 'interesting' is crucial. Above all, this book tries to tell the story of the aerial war in a colloquial and gripping manner, using the art of the story teller as much as the historian's.

If readers have their interest sparked by these words and images then I will be more than happy to see them go off and begin deeper research on their own initiative.

The book tries to recount as much of the story as possible, from the tentative beginnings in the rickety 'birdcages' of 1914 to the fully fledged aerial armadas that swept the skies in 1918. I have tried to look at all sides but, invariably, the main point of view is that of the Royal Flying Corps. This is, perhaps, inevitable considering the writer's own interests and the amount of research material available. I hope readers will not consider it too much of a drawback.

I would like to believe that if there is one thing, more than any other, that comes through in the writing it is my admiration for the brave young men who took to the skies during the Great War. They were pioneers who put their lives at risk every time they settled into their cockpits.

They flew without parachutes and, initially at least, without guns to defend themselves. They flew in aircraft that were built of canvas and wood, aircraft that were more than liable to burst into flames when hit by machine gun fire or when some crucial element in their engines broke. They flew at barely 100 mph and their machines were as vulnerable to the elements as to enemy fire. They flew in open cockpits, in clothing singularly ill-designed to keep them warm and comfortable – frostbite was a not uncommon phenomena in those days.

When all is said and done these men were true heroes who went about their jobs without acclaim and often without recognition. Even star pilots or aces such as Mick Mannock were largely unknown outside the service – in Mannock's case it was not until after the war that the richly deserved but posthumous award of the Victoria Cross was made to the man they called 'King of the Air Fighters'.

Once the pilots and observers reached the Front – men from all of the combatant nations, Allied and Axis alike – they measured their life span in weeks, sometimes even in days. And yet they created a legend that was undiminished throughout the century that followed. They are what this book is really all about.

Phil Carradice
St Athan, August 2011

1
A NEW TYPE OF WAR

On 12 August 1914, less than a fortnight after the outbreak of the Great War, two aircraft passed within a hundred feet of each other in the sky over northern France. They were a German Taube, already nicknamed 'the invisible plane' because the dope used on its wings and fuselage rendered it almost invisible from the ground, and a French single-seater Morane-Saulnier Scout.

It was a beautiful summer day, barely a cloud in the sky. Five thousand feet below the two aircraft, soldiers from both armies were marching and counter marching in the campaign that would soon culminate in the Battle of the Marne.

As yet there were no trenches and the war of movement continued unabated. Despite the advent of machine guns and shrapnel fire from artillery pieces, already there had been such anomalous events as cavalry charges by both sides. The German and the French armies still wore elaborate dress uniforms that made them easy targets for snipers and even regular infantry fire. Only the British in their dirty khaki jackets – the experience of the recent Boer War had clearly been of some use – were really dressed for war. Perhaps most worrying of all, even then – with August not yet played out – there had already been hundreds, maybe even thousands, of casualties on both sides.

High above the killing fields, the two pilots gradually approached each other, waving happily and cheerfully. The men on the ground might be intent on destroying each other but up here it was very different. Neither pilot was armed, not even with a revolver or rifle, and even if they had been, there was little or no inclination on either side to resort to violence.

The job of these aircraft was to monitor troop movements, not fight. Very well, the pilots thought, that is what we shall do. They flew alongside each other for a few minutes, each carefully and surreptitiously noting the lines of the enemy machine. Then, with a final wave, the German pilot pushed over the control column and headed back to his own territory. The Frenchman quickly, with ease and without fuss, did exactly the same.

Such was the way of aerial warfare in August 1914.

* * *

Rumpler Taube *(Bauart Etrich Rumpler),*
erfolgreichstes deutsches Flugzeug.
Es wurden auf diesem Flugzeug der **erste Zuverlässigkeits-
preis am Oberrhein,** *der* **Kathreinerpreis** *(Flug München-
Berlin),* **der grosse Preis von Kiel,** *die* **grösste Gesamtsumme**
vom **B. Z.-Fluge** *und zahlreiche andere Preise gewonnen sowie
verschiedene* **Weltrekorde** *aufgestellt.*

A Rumpler Taube, the main German reconnaissance plane in the early stages of the war, its distinctive dove shape clearly visible in this view taken from below. To begin with the Rumpler, like all early aircraft, was unarmed.

A Morane-Saulnier Scout, used by both British and French forces in the early war years. A later version, introduced in 1916, was known as the Bullet.

On 17 September 1916, ten thousand feet over Cambrai, a German Jagdstaffel led by Oswald Boelcke spots a small formation of British FE 2b fighter-bombers. The Germans are equipped with new Albatross fighters, sleek, shark-shaped aircraft capable of a top speed of over 100 mph and armed with twin synchronised machine guns firing forward through the propeller. Amongst the German formation is a new pilot, a man with a hunter's eye, eager to make his mark and show his skill. His name is Manfred von Richthofen.

Richthofen selects his target and presses home the attack but a series of well-aimed machine gun bursts from the British observer, a young Welshman from Cardiff named Thomas Rees, forces him to break off. Boelcke has lectured his pilots on the 'blind spot' of the FE, however – 'always attack them from beneath', says the master.

Remembering Boelcke's words, Richthofen returns to the fray, zooming up under the tail of the FE. Pressing the trigger buttons of his Spandau machine guns, he rakes the bottom of the British machine, from tail plane to the propeller. The engine is shattered. Smoke and water begin to escape from the engine cowling and the propeller stops. But Richthofen is not finished and another burst pours into the cockpit of the pilot, Lt Lionel Morris. The FE sideslips away, Rees and Morris crumpled and dying in their seats.

By some miracle, Morris recovers consciousness long enough to get the aircraft down to earth. Richthofen, eager to see what has happened, lands in the same field and helps lift the two mortally wounded British airmen from the wrecked machine. Rees opens his eyes, smiles up at the German and dies.

One of the early Albatross biplanes that, with the growth of offensive tactics by both sides, revolutionised aerial warfare.

Richthofen returns to his squadron and immediately writes to a Berlin jeweller asking him to send a silver cup, engraved with the date and the type of plane (he actually gets the type wrong!) to commemorate his first aerial victory.[1] It is something he will do for the next two years.

By September 1916 aerial warfare has clearly changed.

* * *

On the evening of 9 March 1918 Lieutenant Roy Crowden, a young Sopwith Camel pilot who had been at the front for just over a month, settled down in his room to write his diary entry for that day:

> Big aerodrome strafe. We were to bomb Bussigny Aerodrome, sixteen miles over. Also Bristol Fighters, SPADs and SE5s with us. We all met over the aerodrome at two-o-clock – about sixty machines in all. Down we went, shooting like hell. We went down to 400 feet and dropped bombs, 20lb Cooper bombs - - - We kept so low we were on the Huns before they knew it. We charged over the trenches about six feet up and scared the Huns stiff. We made a lot of carts and machines run into ditches – got shot to hell.[2]

The sheer size of the operation, sixty machines in total, was staggering. The logistics involved, just getting the aircraft to the rendezvous on time, and the weaponry needed to carry out the task would have been unthinkable even twelve months before.

Crowden's diary for the next few months was full of entries about ground strafing, diving down, perhaps as low as fifty feet, to machine gun and bomb enemy troops. It was a task for which the Sopwith Camel was eminently suited but was something which all pilots hated. By 23 March he was writing:

> My hat, the fourth job I've done today - - - I'm tired and fed up. Bloody Hun shoots at you from the ground like hell. Not a hope of getting back if he gets your engine at the height we work at. Nothing to eat and no kit – bloody fed up.[3]

In the summer of 1914 no-one could have envisaged aircraft being used in such numbers or in such a way. And certainly nobody could have foreseen the stresses and strains this type of warfare imposed on the airmen.

* * *

Conflict had been simmering between the major powers of Europe for many years before it finally erupted into open warfare in 1914. Nobody envisaged a war of static stalemate, however. To the Generals and to the public of all the combatant nations the expectation was of a war of movement, of flowing

Ground strafing was carried out by most fighter squadrons, a part of the war that the pilots hated and feared with equal ferocity. This view shows a Nieuport 17, a machine gun fixed above the centre section of the wing, in the process of diving on a German factory complex.

cavalry charges across open plains. So, although the fledgling air forces were, to begin with, unknown quantities, it is small wonder that, in time, they came to symbolise an honourable and gentlemanly war, a war of chivalrous conduct and one-to-one combat in the traditional knightly fashion – the opposite to what was happening on the ground and in the trenches. It was a myth, of course. Nothing could have been further from the truth.

By the end of 1918, when the war ended, manned flight had made tremendous strides. It was still only fifteen years since the Wright Brothers first took to the air, a bare seven since Louis Bleriot became the first man to fly across the English Channel. As is often the case, war had advanced technology at an incredible pace and, now, in a period of just over four years, aerial activity – and aerial combat in particular – had altered beyond all recognition.

The last days of October and first few of November 1918 saw what was probably the heaviest air fighting of the whole war. By this time the conflict had turned in favour of the Allies and British bombing raids were continuous, daylight raids designed to support the regular and insistent advance of ground troops and night attacks that were intended to damage or destroy the industrial capabilities of Germany.

The Germans, with resources already shrinking to dangerously low levels, concentrated their aircraft and flew in large formations, trying desperately to protect important strategic centres like railway junctions and factories by the simple process of shooting down the British bombers in large numbers.

British and American Air-Pilots on the Western Front

Allied pilots and observers consulting a trench map before setting out on patrol over German lines.

Three great Jagdgeschwader, led by three skilful pilots – Ernst Udet, Bruno Loerzer and Hermann Goering – took the battle to the British and French air forces. It was not without cost. 30 October was possibly the single worst day with nearly seventy German aircraft destroyed compared to forty-one British.[4] Such losses were, ultimately, unsupportable, particularly for the German Air Force.

In the end it was the weather that stopped the slaughter. As the grey days of November gathered and then closed in across the fields of France, flying became virtually impossible and both sides fell back to enjoy the respite.

It was such a different war from the one experienced by the early airmen of 1914 – not just a different war, it was a different world.

2
THE BEGINNING

When, on the morning of 8 August 1914, thirty-seven frail, ungainly pieces of string and canvas began to flutter precariously over the South Downs, heading for the Channel port of Dover, few of the people who stopped to stare, point and wonder realised that this was almost the total combined might of Britain's operational air fleet.

The important word is 'almost'. There were more aircraft in Britain, of course, over a hundred of them, but they were either damaged and in various states of disrepair or were being used on one of the new rudimentary aerodromes situated in various locations across the southern part of the country. These airfields housed the training schools that were, even then, beginning to turn out pilots and observers by the score.

That morning in August 1914, the thirty-seven aircraft from Nos 2, 3, 4 and 5 Squadrons of the Royal Flying Corps landed in a field on the cliffs above Dover, more or less safely, more or less intact. Some managed to finish up in the drainage ditches that lined the field. These ditches had been marked by flags a day or so before but strong winds had already blown away these markers and the pilots were forced to land 'blind'. Others caught their wheels in the rough terrain and ended up nose down in the earth. But there were no fatalities and by the following day air mechanics had managed to repair most of the damaged aeroplanes.[5]

Over the next few days, as the pilots and aircrew of the fledgling Royal Flying Corps – exotic merely by the nature of what they did – were fêted and entertained in the public houses and taverns of Dover, the air fleet was reinforced by whatever aircraft could be hastily gathered and cobbled together. So when, on 13 August, the armada finally took to the air and headed out across the Channel, the force comprised over sixty aeroplanes.

They were a mixed and bizarre collection, ranging from BE 2s and Avro 504s to French-built Bleriots and Farmans. They were machines that seemed, to the uninitiated, to be held together by glue and bits of string. And so they were. But they were still light years ahead of the aircraft that had begun the aerial revolution barely a dozen years before.

In this early view of British aircraft, a BE2A and a Maurice Farman Longhorn sit side by side on the grass – no tarmac runways then.

EARLY FLIGHT

Man had been fascinated by flight, by the idea of taking to the air like the birds, for thousands of years before the magical moment finally occurred. Legends such as the story of Daedalus and Icarus were known by everyone. There was more, so much more – the designs of Leonardo da Vinci, the visions of sixteenth-century Jesuit priest Francesca Lana who envisaged air machines attacking troops on the ground and the early balloon flights of the Montgolfier Brothers. Flight was a captivating concept that intrigued people of imagination and foresight.

During the eighteenth and nineteenth centuries men often flew in balloons and even in gliders but these machines invariably operated courtesy of the weather – and, to be honest, an awfully large amount of good luck.

Nevertheless, many amazing achievements were still recorded by these intrepid pioneers. In 1836, for example, Charlie Green flew his balloon from London to Germany, a distance of over 500 miles. It was an early world record that was later superseded by John La Mountain's 800-mile journey between St Louis and New York State. And when, in 1849, Franz Uchatius of the Austrian army planned and oversaw a balloon assault on the Italian city of Venice, the age of aerial warfare could be said to have well and truly arrived.[6]

Both the Federal and Confederate armies used balloons during the American Civil War, primarily for observation purposes. And, of course, balloons were used to carry despatches out of the besieged city of Paris during the Franco-Prussian War of 1870–71. Some were shot down but most managed to make their way to safety – one actually managed to travel, battered and buffeted by the wind, as far as northern Norway, a distance of nearly 1,500 miles, before it finally came down to earth.

The achievements of the early balloons and balloonists were so impressive that even the British War Office, always a somewhat reactionary body, was impressed and in 1879 they gave permission for the Royal Engineers to set up a specialist balloon unit. A sum of one hundred and fifty pounds was set aside for the purpose of creating this new detachment.[7]

The idea of powered flight, however, where an aviator or pilot had more control of his own destiny than was ever possible with balloons, was an altogether different concept. It was a difficult and often dangerous undertaking where a simple mistake or an unfortunate gust of wind could cause disaster. It did not stop people trying.

On 2 July 1900 Count Ferdinand Zeppelin made the first controlled flight by a power driven aircraft in Germany when his rigid airship, the sausage shaped LZ 1, flew for nearly twenty minutes over Lake Constance, taking little note of things like the wind and rain showers.

Zeppelin's achievement not only marked the gradual replacement of balloons by airships – a long and fraught process – it also showed that, with further investment and development, the rigid airship might well have a military future.[8] Zeppelin's airships were obviously lighter than air machines

It's 1910 and the Kaiser and Graf von Zeppelin take a stroll, no doubt discussing how best to use airships in the event of war with Britain.

kept afloat by gas-filled bags but they were powered by engines and were thus able to fly, more or less, where their pilots intended them to go.

The German public immediately took Count Zeppelin and his huge airship to their hearts. Yet, in many ways, it was a false dawn. The future of flight lay not with airships but with heavier than air machines, pieces of wood and canvas which, on the face of it and certainly in the eyes of the uninitiated, had little or no business in ever managing to lumber into the sky. People could see the sense in balloons but aircraft with fixed wings and engines were outside their experience and understanding.

Then, on 17 December 1903, two American brothers, bicycle manufacturers by the name of Orville and Wilbur Wright, changed the world. On the salt flats outside the North Carolina town of Kitty Hawk, Orville Wright lay tentatively across the wing of the flimsy Wright Flyer and took to the air, powered by a petrol engine that, these days, would be used simply for a garden mower. It was the world's first heavier-than-air flight.

Orville Wright travelled no more than 120 feet on that first flight but it was a start. The two brothers were almost pathologically secretive about their invention but by 1905 Orville and Wilbur had so improved their machine that on 5 October they were able to fly the incredible distance of 24 miles at a speed of just under 40 mph. From then on progress was rapid.

MAGNIFICENT MEN IN FLYING MACHINES

The first heavier-than-air flight outside the USA was made in 1906 by Albert Santos-Dumont, on open land just outside Paris. The French immediately became the driving force in aircraft development, quickly outstripping all other European nations and, for a while, even the Americans who had given birth to heavier-than-air flight. The new science and technology seemed to suit their mercurial temperament and flying became something of a cult in France.

While in Germany the emphasis remained largely on airships, the first flight in Britain occurred in October 1908. It was achieved by American barnstormer and inventor Samuel Cody, who had come to the United Kingdom with his Wild West Show in 1901. He had been building and flying man-lifting kites, and even balloons, long before the Wright Brothers ever took to the air.

Cody's first flying machine managed a distance of barely a quarter of a mile and though he later went on to build a new plane and win the military sponsored Aeroplane Trials on Salisbury Plain in 1912, his winning design was never put into production for the Royal Flying Corps. Senior RFC officers preferred, instead, the BE2 machine of Geoffrey de Havilland.

Perhaps Cody was too much of an eccentric or loose cannon for the military mind. Whatever the reason, Cody's time in the limelight was limited. He was killed in 1913 when a passenger he was carrying in his machine panicked,

CODY IN FLIGHT

Col CODY

Colonel Cody, American showman and aviation enthusiast, is seen here in one of his aircraft. The first man to fly in Britain, Cody was killed when his plane crashed – supposedly because a passenger panicked and grabbed him around the neck – in 1913, one year before the war began.

grabbed at the pilot's shoulders causing the plane to dive out of control and plough into the ground.[9]

As aircraft developed and became capable of longer and longer flights, intrepid adventurers from all over the world quickly took to the skies. In France, men like Adolphe Pegoud, Jules Vedrines and Louis Bleriot became household names; Pegoud was the first man ever to demonstrate how to 'loop the loop' in Britain. Like many of his contemporaries Pegoud went on to fly in the Great War, becoming one of the first French aces.

Vedrines had an adventurous and chequered career seeming, like many early aviators, to bear a charmed life. On one occasion in 1912 he managed to hit telephone wires and crash as he tried to land. For a time it was feared he would die but he recovered sufficiently to win a two thousand pound prize for the first circuit of Europe and a further four thousand for making the first flight from Paris to Madrid.

British airmen of note included A. V. Roe, more renowned as an aircraft designer than as a pilot, Claude Grahame-White, who created an aerodrome at Hendon in north London, and the famous Cardiff airman B. C. Hucks. Born in Essex, Hucks was the first Englishman to fly upside down and went on to win America's Gordon Bennett Cup. He was one of the early RFC pilots to serve in France but after extensive experience of war flying he was called back to Britain to work as a test pilot for the rest of the war.

B. C. Hucks was born in Essex but based himself, for large parts of his career, in Cardiff. He was one of the early British pioneers of flight – the first Briton ever to fly upside down.

A Maurice Farman Longhorn, shown here during the first year of the war.

On 25 July 1909 French aviator Louis Bleriot scooped them all when he won the *Daily Mail* competition to be the first man to fly across the English Channel. The newspaper had announced the competition earlier in the year, believing and hoping that the winner would be British. It was not to be but Bleriot's achievement, like many of the early aviation successes, owed much to the combined elements of courage and luck.

Bleriot's tiny monoplane was powered by an air-cooled engine that began overheating soon after he left the French coast. Luckily for him he ran into a heavy rain shower over the Channel and this effectively cooled the engine enough for him to complete his flight.

Just a few days before his attempt on the Channel, Bleriot had been badly burned when a petrol line on his aircraft ruptured and he was forced to fly with his legs swathed in bandages. His journey to a field outside Dover, close to the one where the RFC later assembled in August 1914, took just thirty-seven minutes. Britain's long history of splendid isolation had been well and truly breached.

A MILITARY DIMENSION

As aircraft became more reliable so the military brains of the world became more interested in finding out about the new phenomenon and then exploiting what aeroplanes could actually do.

When Graf Zeppelin's LZ4 was destroyed at its moorings in a storm during the late summer of 1908, over six million marks were immediately raised by a German public that had become infatuated with the Count's inventions. It saved the Zeppelin Company and eventually led to a proposal from the General Staff that a fleet of fifteen airships should be built and entered into service with the German Army.[10]

German interest did not stop at airships, however, and in 1912 the German General Staff decided to implement a policy of replacing airships, machines that had previously been used mainly for reconnaissance, with aircraft. The airship fleet would be retained for bombing missions – the start of the Zeppelin Terror that was soon to affect the whole of Britain.

Large sums of money were soon being invested in the promotion and development of aeroplanes and the first German aerodrome was created at Johannisthal outside Berlin. Training of pilots began on 4 July 1910 and the same year no less a person than General Ludendorff went into the air as a passenger. He was impressed enough to lend his support and the purchase of seven aeroplanes for military use was quickly sanctioned.[11]

By 1911 there were fourteen flying schools across Germany as well as two highly significant aircraft factories, those of Albatross and Aviatik. Daimler and Mercedes were producing magnificent water-cooled engines that were already the envy of aircraft manufacturers the world over.

France had always prided itself as being at the forefront of aircraft development. So, when Wilbur Wright travelled to France in 1908 and quickly demonstrated the superiority of his aircraft over anything the French could offer, Gallic pride was hurt. As a consequence, a number of French aircraft factories and flying schools were created where men like Pegout and Vedrines immediately became endowed with all the glamour of modern film stars.

When the value of aircraft as a reconnaissance tool was demonstrated at French military manoeuvres in 1910, orders were placed for twenty Bleriots and twenty Farman two-seaters. It was an ambitious programme but one that clearly indicated French military thinking.

Perhaps more importantly, the Aeronautique Militaire was given a degree of autonomy within the army. General Rocques became Inspector General and quickly set about creating small, self-sufficient units known as escadrilles. By 1912 there were five such units in operation.[12] The aircraft might not have been up to the standard of those in the German Army Air Service but it was, at least, a start.

Britain, of course, took its usual laid back approach to flying. The cavalry had traditionally been regarded as the 'eyes of the army' and with many of the senior officers, both at the War Office and at regimental level, coming from a cavalry background there was a long standing belief that aircraft were nothing more than machines to frighten their horses.

This was despite the fact that in 1911 an official report to the Imperial Defence Committee had commented that aircraft were ideally suited to keep army commanders informed about enemy troop movements. A practical demonstration of their value came during the autumn War Games of 1912 when aircraft on reconnaissance spotted the movements of an army led by no less a commander than Sir Douglas Haig and reported back – with the result that Haig's unit was soundly beaten.[13]

Almost by default, however, the military did begin to inch in the right direction when an Air Battalion of the Royal Engineers was created in April 1911. It was a tiny force, comprising just over 150 men and pilots would have to learn to fly – at their own expense – before applying to join. If they were accepted they would be reimbursed the cost of their training.

A year later, on 13 April 1912, the Air Battalion was disbanded and the larger Royal Flying Corps came into existence. As Quentin Reynolds has noted:

> The infant Royal Flying Corps was born and the Central Flying School established on Salisbury Plain to train men for both army and naval air service. At long last the seed had been planted and it would eventually bring forth a mighty crop.[14]

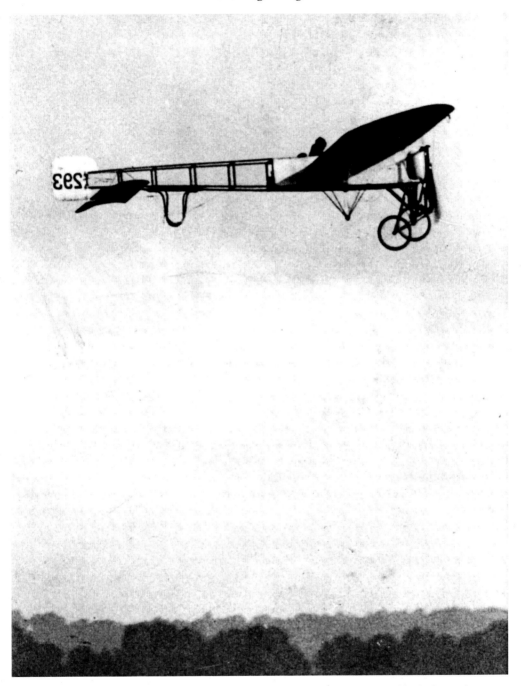

A Bleriot X1 monoplane in flight. Designed by Louis Bleriot himself, this was the machine that carried him across the English Channel in 1909. Many Bleriot monoplanes, single- and two-seater varieties, were used by the RFC in the first months of the war. Bleriot went on to head up and take charge of the famous SPAD Company.

They call us "THE EYES
OF THE ARMY "
For we scout for the foe far and wide,
And with all information worth having
We keep the powers fully supplied –
There are Corps who bear much longer records
For brave deeds, yet History will find
That in the great fight
for the cause of the right,
OUR AIRMEN were not FAR BEHIND.

FROM ONE OF THE

R.F.C.

This postcard shows not just a two-seater Bleriot but also the RFC crest. The poem reads: 'They call us the eyes of the Army/ For we scout for the foe far and wide/ And with all information worth having/ We keep the powers fully supplied.' Hardly great poetry but it sums up the role of the RFC in 1914.

MINOR AIR FORCES, TOO

In the wake of developments in Britain, France and Germany, other countries also quickly established air arms. An Australian Flying Corps was raised in 1913 while the Canadian Aviation Corps came into existence in 1914.

It was March 1911 before Congress in the USA finally voted sufficient funds to develop the tiny American Aeronautical Division (originally founded in 1907) and by 1912 the USA still had only nine military aircraft. This was despite the fact that Glenn Curtiss had effectively demonstrated the effectiveness of aerial bombardment when he dropped dummy bombs on the mock-up of a battleship in June 1910. Little was done to exploit the success and by the time war broke out in 1914 the country that had given birth to heavier-than-air flight had been well and truly left behind in the race for supremacy of the skies.

By 1910 Belgium could boast two airfields and five pilots. Progress was steady rather than spectacular and when the Germans attacked in August 1914 the total flying strength of the Belgian air arm was thirty-eight airmen. They were immediately mobilised, the force being added to by a number of civilian pilots.

The first Italian flying school was created at Centocelle outside Rome in 1910, being quickly followed by six others during the next few months. By the end of the year thirty-one Italian army officers had qualified as pilots.

Italy first used aircraft in combat during the war with Turkey that broke out in September 1911 over the ownership of Libya. Initially, aircraft were used solely

A postcard showing the RFC badge and motto – 'Per Ardua Ad Astra'. The postcard was sent by Jasper Inglis to a girlfriend in Edinburgh, the opening line reading, 'Just a line to let you know I have been transferred to the Royal Flying Corps.'

for reconnaissance but one aeroplane soon carried out a night bombing attack on Turkish positions and in 1912 the enthusiastic Italian public contributed over three million lira towards the purchase of new aircraft for the army.[15]

Russia had been the first nation to use kite balloons in war when several of these strange devices were deployed as part of the defence of Port Arthur in 1904 during the war against Japan. In the wake of the Russian defeat, the Czar's government quickly ordered a number of airships from France and Germany.

Heavier-than-air flight was certainly not ignored by the Russians, either. An Army Central Flying School was established outside St Petersburg in 1910 and over the next few years some fairly revolutionary designs were produced – including an aeroplane, designed for attacking ground forces, with an armoured cockpit that would offer protection to the pilot and observer. Designers like Igor Sikorsky and B. N. Yuriev were instrumental in opening two aircraft factories in St Petersburg. Despite this, the High Command preferred to buy aeroplanes from countries like France and Britain so that by the end of 1913 Russia had 150 fairly modern aircraft available.

Austria-Hungary might still have been considered a major power in the eyes of the world but by 1914 the organisation and infra-structure of the Hapsburg Empire was already beginning to creak. Nowhere was this better illustrated than in the lack of interest in military flying.

Little or nothing was done regarding an Austrian air arm, other than buying a few antiquated flying machines from Germany and, as a consequence, in the early years of the war Austro-Hungarian shortcomings were cruelly exposed by Russian pilots in Galicia. Germany had to shore up her ally by supplying her with large numbers of Aviatik and Rumpler aircraft, machines that could have been more effectively used on the Western Front.

* * *

Such was the state of affairs when war broke out in August 1914. Apart from a few far-sighted individuals, men such as Dutch designer Anthony Fokker, nobody really knew how to use aircraft, other than as a way of watching and then reporting back on the movement of enemy troops. Whether or not aeroplanes would replace the cavalry which, for centuries had assumed the reconnaissance role, was still a matter of conjecture.

With the best will in the world, aircraft were still universally considered odd contraptions that were unreliable and dangerous. The men who flew them? Strange, decidedly strange!

It would take time but over the next few months opinions would change and aircraft would come to be seen as an invaluable weapon, one that would go some way towards actually winning the war. In August 1914, of course, nobody believed this, not even for a moment.

3
AND SO IT BEGINS

At the outbreak of war between Britain and Germany on 4 August 1914 there was little doubt that, out of all the combatants, Germany possessed by far the strongest and most efficient air force. In total they had 246 aircraft and 7 airships – far fewer than the huge fleet of Zeppelins that the press had insisted would soon be raining death and disaster on London and Paris but still enough to cause more than a flicker of alarm in military circles.

Already, Germany had 254 pilots and 271 observers, far more than any of the Allied nations. France had around about 160 aeroplanes, Britain somewhere in the region of 190, although most of these were being used at the training schools that the RFC had recently established.[16]

And even before the RFC crossed to the continent it suffered its first casualties of the war when pilot Robert Skene and Air Mechanic Keith Barlow were killed in a crash shortly after taking off from the aerodrome at Netheravon. It was 12 August and they were en route, first, to Dover and, the following day, to France.

The future pilot and air ace James McCudden, then serving as a mechanic with No. 3 Squadron, witnessed the crash. In fact he started the engine for Skene – one of the first British pilots to have attempted to loop the loop – and watched as the two-seater Bleriot monoplane took to the air. The machine, which had already taken off once and then landed again for some re-adjustments, was flying a little tail heavy, McCudden thought. He watched as it lumbered away over the hangars:

> We then heard the engine stop and following that the awful crash, which once heard is never forgotten. I ran for half a mile and found the machine in a small copse of firs, so I got over the fence and pulled the wreckage away from the occupants, and found them both dead - - - I shall never forget that morning at about half past six, kneeling by poor Keith Barlow and looking at the rising sun and then again at poor Barlow, who had no superficial injury and was killed purely by concussion, and wondering if war was going to be like this always.[17]

When the aircraft of the RFC took off on the morning of 13 August 1914 they were headed, first, for Amiens. Pilots had been ordered to climb to 3,000 feet

An unusual view of a German biplane, taken from above by the observer of another German aircraft. The Maltese crosses are clearly visible on the upper wing, as is the ground far below.

before setting out over the Channel. That way they would be able to glide to safety should their engines fail. Aircraft flew individually with the result that they straggled into Amiens one by one, Major Harvey-Kelly being the first to arrive, shortly before nine o'clock.

THE AIRCRAFT

Looking, now, at the aircraft that made up the warring air forces in 1914 it is hard to imagine how they ever flew, let alone endured combat conditions. But fly they did, for month after month until aircraft development and the requirements of the aerial war rendered them obsolete.

In the summer of 1914 the Royal Flying Corps was equipped with a wide range of machines. At least twenty-three Bleriot monoplanes, single- and two-seater varieties, accompanied the BEF to France that August; aircraft that were more or less similar to the one Bleriot had used to first fly the Channel five years before. After his success, Bleriot had gone on to build over 800 monoplanes, becoming President of the Societe Pour L'Aviation et ses Derives (SPAD for short), and these durable little aeroplanes were well-used by both the British (104 of them being in service with the RFC) and French forces before being withdrawn from active service in the spring of 1915.

The Maurice Farman Longhorn and Shorthorn aircraft – the Longhorn with a long front elevator in front of the cockpit, the Shorthorn without it – were also well used by the RFC. They were 'pusher' aircraft with the engines and propellers being at the back of the machines, behind the pilot and observer. Neither aircraft was particularly well suited to war work and by the middle of 1915 they had been relegated to training duties.

The Avro 504 series of aircraft, built by A. V. Roe, became the main training machine for the RFC, over 8,000 of them being delivered during the war years. There were many versions of the aircraft, ranging from the 504A to the 504K, nearly 300 of them being equipped with a machine gun above the centre section for use against the Zeppelin and Gotha bombers.

A number of early BE2 aircraft had also accompanied the BEF to France and by the end of 1914 the BE2C had become the standard RFC plane. Unfortunately, its very stability – pilots considered it impossible to 'stunt' – made it uniquely ill-suited for combat flying, the machine becoming an easy target for the German fighters. Although largely superseded by the RE8 after 1917, the BE2s continued to be used and by the end of the war there were still over 1,300 of them in service.[18]

The French air force, like the RFC, used many Bleriot monoplanes as well as the ubiquitous Longhorns and Shorthorns in the early – and later – stages of the war. Indeed, they continued to use Shorthorns on the Western Front until the middle of 1917, by which time they were totally obsolete and a death trap for many French aviators.

When the French air service was mobilised in 1914 it boasted twenty-one escadrilles of two-seater Maurice Farman, Caudron and Voison biplanes. A further five escadrilles were soon formed from Dorand aircraft that had been originally destined for export to Russia.

The French-built Morane-Saulnier Scout was a single-seat machine, capable of a top speed of just over 100 mph at 6,500 feet. It was ideally suited to duty as an early fighter plane, being the aircraft that Roland Garros used to obtain his first 'kills'. The aeroplane looked very similar to the German Fokker Eindekker which caused considerable difficulties for anti-aircraft gunners and several of these French machines were undoubtedly peppered with shrapnel from their own side.

Out of the 246 aircraft available to the German air arm in 1914, more than half of them were Taubes, manufactured mainly by the Rumpler Company. These unarmed reconnaissance machines had a clear 'dove' shape, particularly when viewed from above or below. They were capable of climbing to great heights where they were, largely, invisible because of the clear dope used to strengthen their wings and fuselage. A Rumpler Taube had broken the world height record of just under 20,000 feet a few months before war began but, despite this, the aircraft were found to be inadequate for war service and were soon replaced as newer and more effective machines became available to the German air service.

Nevertheless, the future German ace Max Immelmann flew a Taube over Paris in August 1914 and dropped a note calling on the city to surrender.

MAURICE FARMAN BI-PLANE. 40?

A Maurice Farman with the long front elevators clearly evident.

One of the early Avro aircraft with a group of mechanics gathered in front.

An artist's depiction of a duel between a British FE2b and a huge German bomber, probably an Ago pusher machine. The Ago was never very successful, with no more than two dozen ever appearing at the front.

A few months later it was bombs that the Taubes were raining down on British and French forces.

The Fokker Eindekker (E1 version), the creation of Dutch designer Anthony Fokker, was introduced into service during 1914, although it was to be several months later that the aircraft was fitted with a forward firing machine gun, thus making it the world's first true fighter aeroplane.

Some early Albatross, Aviatik and LGV biplanes were available to German forces during the early months of the war but much of the impetus was focussed on the Zeppelin fleet. Great things were expected from these lighter-than-air machines, responsibility for their development and construction being taken over by Dr Arnstein just before war began. The first Zeppelin raid took

The Fokker Eindekker (E1). This revolutionary little machine, when fitted with Anthony Fokker's synchronising gear, became the world's first fighter aircraft. The plane was originally designed as a scout and, like all early aircraft, was originally unarmed.

286. Guerre de 1914-15 — Appareil allemand " Aviatik " descendu par un Aviateur Français
L'H Paris

An Aviatik two-seater, brought down and captured by the French.

place on 25 August 1914 when bombs were dropped on Antwerp, followed several months later by a raid on Britain, but for the Zeppelins it was a slow and steady, rather than spectacular, start to the war.

EARLY DISASTER – AND SUCCESS

In these early days of the conflict, the campaign on the ground was one of rapid movement, of march and counter march, as the Allied forces desperately tried to halt the German thrust into France and Belgium. And although the RFC, on its first trip across the Channel, soon reached Amiens that was as far as it went. For several days pilots simply sat there on the airfield, twiddling their thumbs. Nobody really knew how far Sir John French and the British Expeditionary Force had advanced or where they were based. News from the front did eventually filter back and only at that point were aircraft ordered to Maubeuge, just to the south of Mons.

The planes took off from Amiens on 17 August and almost immediately No. 3 Squadron suffered its second casualty of the war. A BE4, flown by Lieutenant Copland Parry, crashed and caught fire. Parry and his observer, A. M. Parfitt, were burned to death.

Despite the fact that the British pilots had no maps of northern France – they were forced to ask tyre manufacturer Andre Michelin to send them copies of his famous road maps – the RFC began work. Michelin's road maps were practically useless for aerial work but much to the astonishment of the High Command and their own senior officers, the RFC was, from the beginning, highly effective.

The first reconnaissance flights made by the RFC were flown by Philip Joubert de la Ferte and Gilbert Mapplebeck on 19 August, just over two weeks after the outbreak of war. During his flight Mapplebeck passed over a large town which he did not recognise and only on his return to base did he realise he had been over the Belgian capital of Brussels.

On 22 August, Sergeant Major David Jillings became the first British airman to be wounded by enemy fire. He was a large man who had transferred to the RFC from the Guards and was hit by rifle fire from the ground while observing enemy cavalry movements around the Mons area. Unfortunately for Jillings the shot hit him in what was reportedly his very large and fleshy backside – an injury about which his comrades never tired of teasing him. The wound did not damage his career as he rose to be Squadron Leader and win the MC, retiring from the RAF in 1926.[19]

At least Jillings had been hit by enemy fire. At this stage of the war, aircraft had no markings to say which side they came from and often soldiers would take pot shots at any aeroplane that flew overhead. It was a dangerous situation, particularly when aircraft came down low over the battlefield in order to see what was going on.

What it was all about – an aerial photograph showing the Ghent Lys Canal and Grafenburg. Aerial views like this were essential for Generals planning their campaigns and offensives.

To begin with British aeroplanes were painted with Union Jacks, for identification purposes – as shown in this early postcard. The Union Jacks were soon replaced by red, white and blue roundels.

Soon German pilots began to paint black crosses on their aircraft and the British responded by painting Union Jacks on theirs. These were too easily confused with the German Maltese Crosses, however, and were quickly replaced by what became the traditional red, white and blue roundels. French aircraft were also painted with roundels of red and blue.

On the ground the war of movement continued and it was not long before an encircling movement by General von Kluck's First Army was spotted by pilots and observers of No. 5 Squadron. When this was reinforced with further reports, by aircraft from No. 4 Squadron, giving news of troops massing for an attack, Sir John French – despite initial misgivings about the validity of such reports – ordered a strategic withdrawal across the River Marne. The move undoubtedly saved the BEF and French was eternally grateful. He wrote, in an official despatch:

> I wish particularly to bring to your notice the admirable work done by the Royal Flying Corps. Their skill, energy and perseverance have been beyond all praise. They have furnished me with the most complete and accurate information which has been of incalculable value in the conduct of operations.[20]

As the Germans advanced the RFC was forced to abandon its original aerodromes, taking refuge at places such as Le Cateau, La Fere and St Quentin. In those weeks, as the ground war surged around them, pilots and ground crews lived rough, many of the mechanics sleeping under the wings of their aircraft on landing grounds that were usually little more than muddy fields.

The British and French retreat, in the face of overwhelming odds, was often chaotic and confused. Sometimes the pilots and mechanics found themselves in very precarious positions, as James McCudden later recounted. No. 3 Squadron had left its aerodrome at Chantilly and set up a new base at Juilly:

> Late that night we heard the disquieting rumour that there were no British troops between us and the German advanced (sic) guard. A sunken road ran east and west past our landing ground, so all the available mechanics who were left behind with the tenders and machines were armed with rifles, and under the command of Captain Charlton were ordered to hold this sunken road until dawn, when the machines could be flown away.[21]

In the event the Germans did not come that night and McCudden and his comrades were not called upon to fight. With dawn came reinforcements in the shape of a detachment of Irish Horse and No. 3 Squadron was able to get its machines into the air, bound this time for a field at Serris to the south-east of Paris.

Early in September further reports from both British and French aircraft indicated that von Kluck's army, in its haste to reach Paris, had advanced into a long, deep pocket between the French Fifth and Sixth Armies. General 'Pappa' Joffre, commander of the French forces, realised that the decisive moment had come and ordered an attack. The Battle of the Marne lasted for three days and was a bitter and costly affair but it resulted in a French victory and saved Paris. Importantly, without effective aerial reconnaissance the battle would never have been fought, Paris might well have fallen and Germany could well have won the war in 1914.

The Battle of the Marne was followed by a full-scale German withdrawal. When this retreat finally halted along the line of the River Aisne both sides promptly 'dug in', creating a long line of entrenchments that eventually stretched between the North Sea and the Swiss border. For the first time in the war the RFC was able to establish permanent aerodromes where hangars for the aircraft could be built, repair and maintenance facilities could be set up and personnel given comfortable surroundings in which to relax and recuperate.

However, with the war of movement over, it was clear that the role of the air arms, on all sides, would now have to change.

There was no longer any need to record and report on the large scale troop movements that had been typical of the early weeks of the war. Now the requirement was for identifying any activity that might spell a potential build up behind the lines prior to an attack. And, just as important, aircraft could now be used to direct artillery fire and maybe even go on the offensive themselves.

In 1914 very few planes had the equipment to send Morse Code messages but, where and when they did, the results were often spectacular. Reports on the accuracy of shell fire could be sent back within seconds of the explosion and the range or direction of fire could be adjusted accordingly. Very Lights were also used to signal the effect of artillery fire although this was a poor second best when compared to Morse Code.

A stable and reliable aeroplane was required if artillery spotting was to be effective and the RFC had one in the BE2c. This quickly became the standard machine for artillery spotting and reconnaissance duties, replacing the hotchpotch of aircraft that had made up the original force. It took time to replace all the Bleriots, Longhorns and Shorthorns but the RFC in France, under the command of Sir David Henderson, was committed to the task.

One of the most successful operations using spotter planes came, however, not in Europe but above the Rufigi Delta in Africa. The German surface raider *Königsberg* had been causing problems for several weeks, even sinking the light cruiser *Pegasus* outside Zanzibar. Then she was spotted, holed up in the Delta. Two shallow draught monitors, the *Severn* and *Mersey*, managed to cross the sand bar but their gunfire was ineffective with the German ship cleverly camouflaged amongst the trees and wild undergrowth.

Two spotter planes were sent up and, after a detailed search, were able to identify the *Königsberg*. Palm trees had been lashed to her masts and her decks scattered with foliage. Despite this, the planes were able to plot the fall of shells from the monitors and direct their fire. One plane was hit by enemy fire and forced to land but the other remained in the air. Half an hour later the *Königsberg* had been destroyed.

A highly romanticised view of early combat between aircraft. It does, however, show pilots and observers firing rifles and pistols at each other – how aerial combat began.

In 1915 two seaplanes were used to direct fire from the monitors *Severn* and *Mersey* and so destroy the German cruiser *Konigsburg* sheltering in the Rufigi Delta in Africa – a classic case of cooperation between land and air forces.

ARCHIBALD, CERTAINLY NOT

In an attempt to shoot down or discourage the artillery spotting machines both sides soon developed anti-aircraft weapons. The French 75 mm artillery pieces, it was found, could be elevated to a fairly high angle and were duly mounted on the flat beds of lorries as mobile AA batteries.

The early German anti-aircraft guns were 3.7 cm weapons also mounted on trucks and were not particularly effective unless they were firing en masse or against low-flying aircraft. RFC pilots affected to be unmoved by anti-aircraft fire. So the writer W. E. Johns, himself a pilot and creator of the Biggles stories, was happy to make his hero give the following advice to a new pilot:

Watch the sun and never fly straight for more than two minutes at a time
if you can't see what's up in the sun - - - Never mind Archie – it never hits
anything.[22]

German anti-aircraft fire was christened with the derisive nickname 'Archie'
soon after the war began.

The term apparently came from a comment made by Lt 'Biffy' Borton of No.
5 Squadron. He would greet inaccurate fire by singing out 'Archibald, certainly
not!' The phrase came from a George Robey song where a philandering
husband was greeted by the jibe whenever he chanced his arm. Within weeks
the term was common parlance throughout the RFC and remained in use until
the outbreak of the Second World War.

Anti-aircraft fire, however, could be highly effective, particularly as the war
went on and equipment improved. Much to the chagrin of pilots, its accuracy
increased alarmingly when planes were engaged in low flying operations.
Despite this, many pilots greeted Archie like an old friend whose familiarity
was both reassuring and useful. As German Archie burst with black smoke,
British and French with white, many pilots soon learned to use the bursts as a
way of indicating when there were enemy or friendly aircraft in the immediate
vicinity – a more than useful way of 'watching your back'.

THE OFFENSIVE SPIRIT

The Flying Corps had achieved its first combat victory on 26 August 1914.
After flying over the British aerodrome at Le Cateau, where James McCudden
took a pot shot at the enemy aircraft with his pistol – he missed – a German
Rumpler Taube was forced down by Lt Harvey-Kelly and two colleagues.
Following Harvey-Kelly's lead, the British planes simply flew closer and closer
to the Taube until he, literally, ran out of air and was forced to land. The
British pilots set fire to the German machine but the enemy airmen managed
to escape.

The success of aerial reconnaissance and artillery spotting soon made it clear
that forcing down enemy aircraft – or at least forcing them to abandon their
mission – had become an essential part of the war in the air. Consequently,
pilots and observers began to arm themselves with rifles and pistols and, by
autumn, firing at enemy aircraft had become the norm, not the exception.

Lt Louis Strange even mounted a machine gun in his observer's cockpit, but
its weight seriously restricted the speed and ceiling of his Maurice Farman
Shorthorn. His commanding officer promptly ordered Strange to remove the
gun and content himself with a rifle. Strange, always an innovator, was not
happy and when a French pilot, firing a machine gun, brought down a German
plane that October, he decided to try once more. When he shot down an Aviatik

GUERRE AERIENNE – Canon employé par les Allemands pour tirer contre les aéroplanes
AERIAL WAR – Gun employed by the Germans for firing at the aeroplanes

Visé, Paris

A German anti-aircraft gun – Archie, as it was affectionately called by British pilots.

CAMPAGNE DE 1914-1915

Visé Paris N° 535

Automobile blindée, tir contre Aéroplanes.

ND. Phot.

A mobile French Archie battery, machine guns mounted on the back of a truck. Machine guns were always more effective against aircraft than shells but only when the planes were flying low.

Members of the RFC practice with machine guns, ready to defend their aerodrome. A tripod has been improvised in order to help the men with their accuracy.

on 14 November, Strange felt more than vindicated and was not afraid to say so.

With permanent aerodromes now available to them, on either side of the lines, French, German and British pilots began to come under pressure to carry out short-range bombing missions. Sometimes they hurled early versions of hand grenades from their pockets. It was estimated that an airman had approximately eight seconds to get rid of the grenade once the pin was pulled – certainly not an easy task in an aeroplane that was rocking and swaying through the air.

The French airmen used something called a flechette. It was simply a tin that held a number of steel arrows which scattered once the tin was thrown over the side of the aeroplane. Flechettes were also used by some RFC pilots but, in general, they found a far better use in RFC messes – as darts.[23]

Early bombing raids were, literally, hit or miss affairs. Bomb sights were things of the future and there was no way of aiming bombs. As a consequence, the missiles rarely fell on their intended targets. Nevertheless, pilots and observers tried their best, often carrying eight and ten pound bombs in their cockpits – a lethal situation at the best of times.

Lieutenant Louis Strange, one of the early exponents of machine guns in aircraft – his efforts were met with official disapproval. Sometime later Strange had one of the luckiest escapes in the war when he was flung from his plane in mid-air, but managed to hold on and regain control.

An early bomb is despatched at the Germans – hand held and with a message scrawled on the side.

French airmen pose with a dart bomb. Never the most effective of weapons, the French loved dropping them on enemy positions – it was more the thought of what they might do than the actual efficiency of the weapons.

NO SIGN OF WAR

For most pilots, however, flying in these early months of the war was just that – flying. The war was a long way away and rarely intruded on the pleasures of taking to the air. Indeed, more discomfort came from the problems of inhaling the castor oil burnt by aircraft like the Caudron – with the fairly obvious but rarely mentioned consequence – than from Archie or enemy machines.

Duncan Grinnel-Milne later remembered his early days of flying in France with more than a little degree of nostalgia:

> In the main the country was flat and much broken up by ditches and small streams. Innumerable strips of cultivated land made a good natural camouflage, rendering observation difficult. I saw a man and two horses ploughing, some cows grazing, a farm cart being driven down a narrow track, a toy train puffing along a thread-like railway. But there were no large scale movements and, save to the east, no signs of war.[24]

For most of the young pilots – the old hands, the pre-war flyers, were soon despatched home to training squadrons and advisory posts – it was a time to gain confidence in their new skills, to come to terms with the sudden power and freedom with which they had been suddenly imbued:

> In those days I lived for the air. There was nothing in life to compare with taking a machine off the ground, wheeling away into the sky, trying turns,

One of the early BE type aircraft – note the mechanic preparing to swing the prop.

spirals, dives, stalls, gliding, zooming, doing all the stunts a pilot needs to give him confidence and nerve in a tight corner.[25]

Of course there were moments of high drama and tragedy but nothing to compare to the mayhem that would come in the months and years ahead. It was, in many respects, something of an interregnum.

THE ROYAL NAVAL AIR SERVICE

The British Admiralty had long had an interest in the potential benefits of flight. So much so that even before the Royal Flying Corps was founded in 1912 a group of naval aviators had already established a flying school on the Isle of Sheppey. Winston Churchill, First Lord of the Admiralty, was an enthusiastic supporter of this naval wing and had actually taken to the air himself. Under his guidance and prompting, trials and investigations were soon being made regarding ways of launching bombing attacks on shipping.

The creation of the RFC was intended to bring together the aviators of the Air Battalion and the naval wing but things did not work out quite that way:

The Admiralty was not keen to hand control of its flying matters over to an army corps. It therefore rejected the idea of a 'naval wing' and announced the formation of the Royal Naval Air Service, under the command of Murray Sueter.[26]

100.

The King inspecting R.N.A.S Officers

Official Photograph—Crown Copyright reserved

"Daily Mail" War Pictures

The King inspects a detachment of RNAS officers somewhere in France. Much of the early fighting was carried out by the RNAS, the service being imbued with the offensive spirit.

Willows 4, one of several airships bought from private individuals at the start of the war. Ernest Willows was paid one thousand pounds for his balloon.

It took several years for the Royal Naval Air Service to become a reality and it was July 1914 before the Service actually came into existence. But from the beginning the Admiralty was more interested in offensive operations than it was with reconnaissance. The Admiralty was only too aware that their naval bases along the coast of Britain might be vulnerable to attack from Zeppelin bases on the Continent and so they created a series of air stations in the south-east of the country. From these new air stations, it was felt, the RNAS would be able to launch attacks on any raiders who might approach and, more importantly, undertake strategic raids against enemy bases to prevent any such attacks happening in the first place.

By 4 August 1914 the RNAS consisted of just over fifty seaplanes, several of them fitted with wireless telegraphy equipment which could keep the aircraft in touch with their base. There were also seven airships, one of which – the Willows 4 – had been purchased from Cardiff balloonist Ernest Willows. With 43 flying officers, 91 other officers and nearly 700 enlisted men the Service was certainly well equipped to carry out its primary purpose – to defend the east coast of Britain and to protect shipping in the English Channel.[27]

THE RNAS AT WAR

When it became clear that there would be no immediate German invasion of Britain, Sir David Henderson of the RFC and Winston Churchill of the Admiralty agreed that units of the RNAS might be of more use in France and Belgium than sitting, waiting for action on the east coast of England. The squadron previously based at Eastchurch had already been operating out of Ostend but when the town was taken by the Germans they were transferred to Dunkirk with the orders to keep enemy aircraft and Zeppelins away from the port and its immediate environs.

The Eastchurch Squadron was commanded by Charles Rumney Samson, a very experienced and capable airman. Enormously popular with his men, Samson was a man of action and when bad weather grounded his aircraft he decided to use armoured cars – many of which he built and designed himself – to go out and search for enemy units.

Twenty miles outside Dunkirk, Samson encountered a German car containing a number of staff officers. He immediately opened fire with the Maxim gun he had mounted on the armoured car and sent the enemy scuttling away. More importantly, they went with the distinct impression that Dunkirk was occupied by a large force of British soldiers and Marines.

Pleased with the results of Samson's enterprise, Churchill promptly reinforced the Eastchurch Squadron with more armoured cars, several aircraft and another 250 Marines. Over the next few weeks Samson developed a system where his spotter aircraft would locate enemy units and wireless back

Charles Samson and a group of fellow airmen. Already renowned as a pilot before the war began, Samson used armoured cars to take the war to the Germans.

An armoured car, as used by Samson and his RNAS detachment.

On 21 November 1914 three British airmen from the RNAS, Briggs, Babington and Sippe, attacked the giant Zeppelin sheds at Friedrichshaven, causing considerable damage.

their location. Samson and his armoured cars would then head off to intercept and, if possible, destroy the German force.

Samson also planned and operated reconnaissance and bombing raids. A series of attacks on the Zeppelin sheds at Dusseldorf and Cologne were initially unsuccessful but they were quickly followed by further attacks on the two German bases. These were carried out by Flight Lieutenant Reginald Marix and Squadron Commander Spenser Grey.

Grey managed to drop his bombs on the main railway station at Cologne, causing considerable damage and disruption. Flying at 600 feet, Marix then swept in across the Zeppelin shed at Dusseldorf and dropped two twenty pound bombs directly onto the roof. The shed burst into flames, sending a

On 8 October 1914, Douglas Spencer Grey led a raid on Cologne, flying almost 200 miles into Germany to destroy part of the railway station. This artist's impression shows Grey high above the famous Cologne Cathedral.

Another RNAS bombing raid took place on Christmas Day 1914, when nine seaplanes attacked the German Naval Base at Cuxhaven.

wall of flame into the sky and totally destroying the recently completed Z 19 that was sitting inside. Matrix managed to get within twenty miles of his base before his Sopwith Tabloid, hit in over fifty places, was forced to land. He simply borrowed a bicycle and rode back home, having completed the first ever successful bombing attack on German territory.[28]

On Christmas Day 1914 – while troops along the line were engaged in their unofficial truce – the RNAS undertook a further raid on Cuxhaven naval base. The raid was carried out by nine seaplanes that had been transported to the German coast and then lowered into the sea for take-off. Most of the bombs missed their target but the raid did, at least, force the German Navy to disperse its fleet along the full length of the Kiel Canal.

4

TRAINING

It is a sad fact that over 14,000 airmen lost their lives during the Great War. Amazingly, over 8,000 of these fatalities came from accidents during training. Such statistics were hardly surprising as instructors were often no better trained or experienced than the men they were teaching and the aircraft they used were invariably obsolete, difficult to fly and liable to break up under any undue strain.

Britain may have been slow to latch on to the value of aircraft but the situation did not last. In the autumn of 1914, with the need for trained pilots clear to everyone, the Central Flying School at Upavon on Salisbury Plain was greatly extended and several civilian flying schools were bought for military use. These included Brooklands, Gosport and Hounslow. New training centres were established at places like Castle Bromwich, Catterick and Northolt.

Training remained pretty basic, however, as Duncan Grinnell-Milne was later to recount:

> I stared forward helplessly, hopelessly. The machine was bounding over a stretch of uneven ground, swinging wildly from side to side. Which rudder had he told me to use? Left or right? I tried each in turn, gradually discovering how to keep the nose straight while fumbling around with my left hand to find the switch. My fingers encountered the throttle lever, pushed it forward - - - the engine roared with satisfaction. The tail came off the ground, I felt myself being lifted in my seat - - - The bumping and bounding suddenly ceased – merciful heavens, I was off the ground.[29]

The first solo flight was a trial for every pilot but was no worse than the early dual flights where the trainee had no means of communication with his instructor – apart from hand signals or bellowed messages that were invariably whipped away by the wind – and often had to cling on for dear life, without seat belt or any means of keeping him inside the aeroplane should the machine suddenly bank or dip its wings.

The first stage was for a trainee pilot to 'take his ticket', in other words undergoing a practical test set and carried out by the Royal Aero Club. Once this had been successfully attained – and the test was not always rigorously

French soldiers gather around a crashed Allied aircraft, *c.* 1916.

An incident from 1915. This is an artist's impression of Lt Vernon attempting to retrieve valuable documents from a downed German plane – German artillery tries to prevent him.

applied – the next step was to report to an 'advanced' school like Gosport or Upavon where the intention was to prepare the pilot for the war in France.

In December 1916 Major Robert Smith-Barry took charge of the training school at Gosport. He revolutionised pilot training, insisting that his instructors teach their pupils useful tricks, like how to get out of a spin. Using the Avro 504K, his aim was to help pilots survive over the Western Front, something he achieved with a fair degree of success. In the early days of the war, however, such techniques could only be learned in one place – at the front.

By the end of 1915 Germany had a grand total of twenty operational flying schools, turning out pilots for reconnaissance, bombing and, increasingly, for the new fighter Squadrons. Four special schools for the training of artillery spotters were also in existence. With the German policy at this time of having officers as observers – and therefore in charge of the aircraft – the pilots were invariably NCOs, in effect aerial chauffeurs. So when a Prussian officer like Baron Manfred von Richthofen applied to join the Flying Service he was, initially, trained as an observer.

Richthofen arrived at Air Replacement Station 7, outside Cologne, to begin his training on 6 June 1915:

Naturally, I was anxious to get to the Front. I was afraid I would get there too late and that the war might be over. I had to spend three months to train as an observer; at the end of that time peace might have been concluded. Thus,

Manfred von Richthofen, the greatest air ace of the war, a rather romanticised picture produced as a piece of propaganda.

it never occurred to me to train as a pilot. I felt that, due to my training as a cavalry man, I would do well as an observer.[30]

Changes were also taking place in the French air service. Key information given to him prior to the Battle of the Marne had convinced General Joffre of the value of aerial reconnaissance. As a consequence, he ordered Commandant Bares to reorganise and expand the French Aeronautique Militaire. By 8 October 1914 a proposal for no fewer than sixty-five escadrilles had been created. These were broken down into escadrilles de chase (in effect fighter squadrons) flying the Morane-Saulnier monoplanes, escadrilles de corps to undertake artillery spotting and reconnaissance duties and, finally, escadrilles de bombardment to take the war to the enemy.

NOT JUST PILOTS

In order for the aircraft of both sides to take to the air a huge support infrastructure, ranging from the provision of hangars and spare parts to obtaining petrol supplies and replacement aeroplanes, had to be deployed. In particular there was the job of training and organising the ground staff whose simple but crucial task was to keep the aircraft flying.

With the RFC in France under the command of Sir David Henderson, it was left to General Hugh Trenchard and Captain Sefton-Brancker to build up and run the British supply networks. Sefton-Brancker quickly enlisted every mechanic he could find in order to keep aircraft in the air.

All members of the various air arms were tradesmen, roughly divided into riggers and fitters. Riggers spent their time on the actual body or air frame of the aircraft, mending struts and bracing wires, plugging holes in the flimsy canvas structures. Fitters were mechanics whose job was to ensure the engines worked effectively.

Basic training normally lasted for three months, followed by a further three months of intensive training. In the RFC, during the period of basic training, each rigger also carried out the work of the fitters while each fitter carried out the tasks normally allotted to the riggers. It was a useful exercise as, once attached to a Squadron, the men would often have to turn their hands to any task that needed to be done, everything from stretching and doping fabric to replacing engine parts and filling tanks with petrol.

It usually meant long, arduous hours of thankless work – and often it was dangerous as well. James McCudden, the future ace, wrote about one experience when he was called on to lend assistance to an aircraft that had come down just short of the lines:

Mr Conran had landed near the village of Montreuil on the north of the Marne, just behind our infantry, and I had to go forward to be of assistance

An unknown mechanic poses for the camera.

Ground crew – mechanics and riggers – were the unsung heroes of all the flying services. Without them the aircraft simply would not fly.

A group of mechanics working on a rotary engine, *c.* 1915.

Aircraft were valuable commodities – one of the reasons parachutes were not issued to airmen as it was feared pilots would jump out of damaged machines rather than nurse them back to base. So when an aircraft came down close to the lines mechanics would often have to go forward and repair the machine under fire.

- - - At last I found the Parasol Bleriot, and filled it with some more petrol and oil - - - I went in Major Salmond's car. I had to sit with a loaded rifle across my knees in the car as we were close on the heels of the German rearguard and there were several small uncaptured detachments at large in the numerous copses and woods.[31]

The pilot, Lieutenant Conran – the man who had spotted the German moves against the BEF and enabled the retreat from Mons to be successfully completed – was able to climb into his aircraft and fly back to the aerodrome. McCudden did not have such luxury and had to make the journey by car. When he returned to his Squadron, McCudden resumed his normal duties as if nothing had happened, pausing only to grab a quick meal:

After replenishing the inner man I worked all night on the engine of the Parasol, cleaning and grinding in the inlet valves, and also fitting new inlet valve springs.[32]

McCudden's adventure was not unusual. Similar missions were repeated many times, by pilots and ground crew of the RFC. Saving aircraft, wherever and whenever possible, was always crucially important.

CAMP D'AVIATION, près DIJON — Les Hangars

The French aerodrome at Dijon, a typical air base with wooden hangars. The German air service, by contrast, often housed their planes in large tents.

A group of German mechanics in front of their aircraft.

ORGANISATION

Invariably, with aircraft suddenly providing a new dimension to warfare, there was much organisation and re-organisation on both sides of the lines as events progressed and the war ground mercilessly on.

A lull in the fighting during the winter of 1914/15 gave the RFC the opportunity to assess its performance. One of the first things noticed by far-sighted men like Hugh (or Boom as he was known in the RFC) Trenchard was the urgent need for Squadrons to be equipped, not by a hotchpotch of various aircraft but with planes of similar make and performance. At this early stage the idea of homogenous units lay some way in the future. But it was an aim, an ideal, and men like Trenchard were intent on making it a reality.

At the end of October, Wings – each of three or four Squadrons – were created and attached to the various Army Corps then operating in France. It was an administrative change, one that made the aerial war much easier to run but did not really affect the day to day routines in the Squadrons. Trenchard was allocated No. 1 Wing.

By March 1915 the RFC had eight Squadrons in France but, unfortunately, the aircraft in these units were comprised of no fewer than twelve different types. It was not until July 1915 that the first homogenous unit, No. 11 Squadron, arrived with its new DH2 aeroplanes.[33]

David Henderson, the original commander of the RFC in France.

Sir Hugh 'Boom' Trenchard, the man credited as being the founder of the RAF. A far-sighted and intractable man, he later went on to command the Independent Air Force and take full control of the RAF in the post-war years.

A further re-organisation came in January 1916 when each of the British Armies was given two Wings, an Army Wing – capable of long range missions into enemy territory – and a Corps Wing that undertook reconnaissance and artillery spotting tasks. By the summer of 1916, the RFC had twenty-seven Squadrons operating in France, now under the overall command of Sir Hugh Trenchard, who had taken over control of the Flying Corps from David Henderson in August 1915.

There was a near-disaster for the French Aeronautique Militaire in the summer of 1914 when General Bernard – convinced that the war would end quickly – closed down all the French flying schools (an action that was soon rescinded). Despite this blunder, by October 1914 the French had totally reorganised their air service, aiming for a total of 119 escadrilles.

By the opening days of the Battle of Verdun the French could boast 1,149 aircraft. It was unfortunate that the majority of these aeroplanes were already obsolete. The only modern unit in the French air force, flying Nieuport biplanes, was a special group put together from the best pilots in all the other escadrilles, a unit that later achieved fame as Les Cicognes, the Stork Escadrille.

The situation was soon to change with the advent of a number of fine new fighters then beginning to enter service. Most notable among these were the Nieuport 17, favourite of British aces like Albert Ball and Mick Mannock, and the redoubtable SPAD 17, on which Georges Guynemer achieved virtually all of his fifty-four victories.

To begin with the various German Squadrons had operated in total isolation from each other. It soon became apparent, however, that close co-operation between the various units was essential and by the end of 1914 a Staff Officer for Aviation had been appointed to each army headquarters.

By the spring of 1915, following the success of the Fokker Eindekker – the world's first true fighter plane – a number of 'Battle Wings' had been established and Hauptman Thomsen of the German General Staff was already advocating the formation of a third service, an air force that would augment the work of the Army and Kriegsmarine. Nothing came of Thomsen's recommendations but in 1916 the creation of powerful Jagdstaffeln (Jastas as they were known), powerful mobile fighting units, were beginning to cause major problems for the Allies.

By the middle of 1916 it was clear that the German Air Force had become a significant military unit. Ernst von Hoeppner was appointed General Commanding the Air Service on 8 October 1916, responsible only to the Commander in Chief. Under Hoeppner, the Jastas were given free rein to roam the battlefront, shooting down the Allied fighters so that the German reconnaissance machines could go about their business without interference.[34]

Regular re-organisation of the air arms of all the combatant nations continued until the end of the war. By November 1918 the air war and the means to wage it had altered out of all proportions. The pilots and ground crews of 1914 and 1915 would never have recognised it.

British pilots check their maps and the position of the trenches before setting out on another patrol.

WHO WERE THESE MEN?

The pilots, observers and ground crews who made up the various air forces were a new breed of men. They were invariably young and eager for adventure. They were interested in new technologies and they knew that they took their lives in their hands each time they went up into the air.

Almost without fail, they loved taking risks. They would, these days, probably be men who engaged in extreme sports and while they needed a certain degree of academic or technical ability, the desire to push at the boundaries, to stretch themselves to the limits, was always more important than classroom study. Manfred von Richthofen summed up the attitudes of so many pilots when he wrote about his early days in the German Cadet Corps:

I was never good at learning things. I did just enough work to pass. In my opinion, it would have been wrong to do more than was necessary, so I worked as little as possible - - - I had a great liking for risky tricks. One fine day my friend Frankenberg and I climbed the well-known steeple of Wahlstatt by going up the lightning rod. I tied my handkerchief to the top of the steeple. I remember vividly how difficult it had been to negotiate the gutters along the way.[35]

Many of these early airmen went on to achieve fame and immortality, amassing huge victory tallies and becoming legends in their own lifetimes. Men like Richthofen, Udet, Boelcke, Mannock, McCudden, Fonck and Guynemer established reputations that have stood the test of time.

Yet these were only the tip of the iceberg. Other pilots burned brightly and quickly and then, like moths dancing too close to the flames, disappeared from view. Yet they, as much as Richthofen, Mannock and the rest, were instrumental in creating the legend of the aerial fighters of the Great War.

Pilots like Lieutenant Benjamin Thomas might have shot down only three enemy aircraft but he was typical of the rank and file airmen serving on the Western Front. His combat report for one of these kills, laconic and almost matter-of-fact, reads as follows:

> We encountered a large formation of EA scouts above us and to the east - - - I noticed two Fokkers detached from their formation and much lower. I picked out one and fired about 100 rounds at an approximate range of 150 yards. The EA immediately went down out of control and was seen to crash by my observer, just south of Cambrai.[36]

Just a few weeks after recording this victory, Benjamin Thomas was killed as he returned from the Dawn Patrol when his Bristol Fighter was involved in a mid-air collision with another plane from the same Squadron.

The pilots of all the air services knew that they led a dangerous existence. They embraced it and tried to follow the advice of the legendary eighteenth-century pirate Black Bart Roberts – 'A short life but a merry one!'

In the main – and on the surface, at least – they served with a light heart, trying hard to convince themselves that they would see the war through to a successful conclusion. The reality was very different. Frank Owen, a Sergeant gunner/observer on a DH9 Squadron, sent a typical, upbeat message to his sister and brother-in-law, telling them that he had just transferred to flying duties:

> Well, dear Sarah, the Kaiser will be astonished when he learns that Frank Owen has joined the Flying Corps. I guess he'll tell the German airmen to be careful and keep their eyes skinned or Frank will be there first.[37]

Owen had already won the DCM serving in the trenches with the Royal Engineers when he picked up and flung a grenade back over the parapet, saving dozens of lives in the process. Yet even he had his moments of worry and doubt:

> I've got such a queer presentiment that now and again makes me feel a bit down. I seem to think that the next time I go to France will be the last.[38]

Frank Owen was right to worry. On 1 October 1918 his DH9 was shot down while on a bombing raid over enemy territory. Owen was killed instantly.

Fear was inevitable; men wouldn't have been human without it. And as a pilot's tour of duty progressed, as nerves began to fray and shatter, it became harder and harder to push it away. When Roy Crowden first joined 54 Squadron he was proud, happy and enthusiastic:

> Ah ha! Dirty work at the cross roads. My first scrap today. Thank heavens I wasn't frightened but quite enjoyed it. Patrol eight strong – feel like sweeping the sky with such strength. Hun Archie was going like Hell. Found a piece in my top plane when I landed. Damned excited.[39]

Five months later, after the deaths of many friends and colleagues, it was a very different matter for the young man:

> Not a Hun in the sky and now I am feeling absolutely awful. I very nearly fainted in the air. I am going to the CO about it. I simply can't stick any

An incident high above the Flanders mud. A German Aviatik 'surrenders' to a British FE2b – a drawing originally published in a British magazine of the time.

more high stuff. Our front these days is anywhere between Rhiems, Chateau Thiery and Soissons.[40]

The pilots and observers, of course, were only part of the picture. Corporal G. R. Butt was medically examined at New Scotland Yard in December 1915 and after training at Filton in Bristol, was sent to join No. 19 Squadron. As well as serving as an Air Mechanic, Butt flew occasionally as an observer. This was a fairly common occurrence – it was, after all, how McCudden gained his early experience of war flying. Butt was no different and his diary gives a graphic description of life at an RFC aerodrome:

8th Aug – Bradley shot down.
24th Aug – Henderson shot down.
27th Aug – Reynall, Callaghan, Talbot, Briggs and Corbold all missing.
2nd Sept – Johnson wounded – also Downing.[41]

While several of the five pilots Butt listed as missing on 27 August later turned up, having been forced down closer to the lines, the diary entry does show the dangers involved in early war flying – and the almost negligent way in which it was treated. It was the only way to cope with perpetual danger, when death was ever-present and empty chairs in the Mess of an evening were the expectation rather than unusual.

The inclination to ignore danger, to treat it simply as an occupational hazard, was essential in the development of a pilot's character. Men of the RFC even sang about it:

The young aviator lay dying as 'neath the wreckage he lay.
To the Ak Emmas around him assembled, these last parting words he did say:
Take the cylinder out of my kidney, the connecting rod out of my brain,
From the small of my back take the crankshaft and assemble the engine again.[42]

The RFC tradition of never mourning a lost comrade but, instead, of carrying on regardless was not an affectation. It was an essential part of the survival process in times of war.

5

THE FIRST FIGHTER

In April 1915, a flight of four German reconnaissance planes patrolling high over the French lines were startled by the sudden appearance of a sleek Morane-Saulnier scout. The German pilots were not unduly worried until bright flames began to spurt from the single machine gun mounted behind the propeller of the French aircraft and bullets began slamming into their wings and fuselage. Within minutes two of the German machines had plummeted down in flames, the other two had fled. The age of the fighter had arrived.

The French pilot was none other than Roland Garros, one of the famous pre-war flyers who had amazed the world with his acrobatics and aerial stunts. Now, by firing forward through his propeller, Garros had done it again, he had taken the war in the air to a new level.

It made sense for a gun to fire along the pilot's line of sight. It meant that all the airman had to do was to point his machine at the enemy aircraft and pull the trigger. But how to achieve such a miracle without blowing off your own propeller was a major obstacle.

In fact, before the war had even begun, Raymond Saulnier of France and Franz Schneider in Germany had both designed interrupter gears to allow this to happen. But the gears were unreliable, the machinery heavy and, almost as a way of 'making assurance double sure', Saulnier fitted triangular deflector plates to the propeller of any plane that used his invention. It was a basic principle – the gun would fire and any rounds that hit the propeller would simply be deflected.

Garros quickly discarded the heavy interrupter gear, relying on his skill and manoeuvrability to get into the right position and on the deflector blades to protect his propeller from any errant rounds.

It was a risky business at the best of times as this type of warfare was not an exact science. There were many inherent dangers in what he was doing – shooting off his propeller was just one possibility. Engine failure caused by the vibrations of bullets hitting the blades was another. And then, of course, there was the simple but very real possibility of a stray bullet bouncing back off the deflector blades and hitting the pilot.

Nevertheless, for three weeks Garros cut a swathe through the German Air Force, sending six enemy machines down in flames. Then the inevitable

French ace Vedrines is shown here in his Morane scout. Note the deflector blades on the propeller.

happened. Engine failure forced him down behind the German lines and before he could destroy his machine he was captured by an infantry detachment. Even as Garros was wined and dined at the nearest aerodrome – with all the civility normally shown to captured enemy pilots – German technicians were eagerly examining his plane.

Realising that they were faced by a revolutionary device that could so easily change the course of the aerial war, Garros' little monoplane was immediately sent to Berlin, along with the message – design something similar for us!

ENTER ANTHONY FOKKER

Anthony Fokker was a Dutchman who had become obsessed with aircraft at an early age. Indeed, he built his first aeroplane when he was just sixteen years old, in the kitchen of his parents' house in Haarlem on the Dutch coast.

When, at the age of twenty, Fokker designed a brand new monoplane, he was distraught to find that the Dutch government had no interest in his invention. He tried to 'peddle' it to Russia, France and England but without success. Only in 1913, when he turned to Germany, demonstrating his machine by looping-the-loop and earning himself the sobriquet of 'The Flying Dutchman', did success finally loom.[43]

Fokker was quickly established in a factory at Schwerin, 200 miles away from Berlin, with a contract to design a dozen reconnaissance aircraft for

Anthony Fokker, the brilliantly gifted young Dutchman who built planes for Germany. He had previously offered his serviced to Holland, France and Britain but had been turned down.

the German Army. When war broke out, Fokker continued to work for the German government, despite the fact that Holland remained neutral.

He might have been politically naïve but there was no doubt that the aircraft Fokker was producing were both reliable and effective. Fokker's single wing E1 scout, the Eindekker as it was known, was highly regarded as a fast and manoeuvrable aircraft and German pilots, armed with rifles and revolvers, were quickly making a nuisance of themselves on the Western Front.

Anthony Fokker was the man to whom the German High Command now turned. As it happened, he had already been tinkering with an idea for forward-firing machine guns and within two days he had designed a revolutionary synchronising gear that enabled machine gun bullets to be fired between the blades of a propeller.

Legend says that Fokker found his inspiration by drawing on his memory of the blades of Dutch windmills which revolved constantly and through which he and his school friends would throw stones, without ever hitting the blades. It makes a lovely story but regardless of whether or not it is true, Fokker was soon calling German officials to come and witness his device in action.

The device was fitted to Fokker's E1 monoplane and, when demonstrated – both on the ground and in the air – was found to work perfectly. Then came orders from Berlin – Fokker was to take his plane and synchroniser gear to the Front and demonstrate its effectiveness by shooting down an enemy plane.

Fokker's protests about neutrality were ignored. He was given a uniform and an identification card declaring him to be a member of the German armed

An early postcard showing how pilots were able to fire through the propeller without killing themselves – although it is doubtful if anyone who bought the card had the faintest understanding about what it was describing.

forces and, almost before he knew it, he found himself in the air above the trenches. He soon encountered a French Maurice Farman two-seater and knew that he could destroy the enemy machine in a matter of seconds:

> I had my finger on the trigger - - - The French pilots were watching me curiously. In another instant, it would be all over for them. Suddenly I decided that the whole job could go to hell. It was too much like 'cold meat' to suit me. I had no stomach for the whole business, nor any wish to kill Frenchmen for Germans. Let them do their own killing.[44]

Fokker returned to the aerodrome, told the authorities what he decided and set off for Berlin. Still keen to see what it could do, the High Command gave the aircraft and its synchronising device to Lieutenant Oswald Boelcke and, a day later, he brought down his first victim. A few days later Lieutenant Max Immelmann repeated the feat.

THE FOKKER SCOURGE

Anthony Fokker immediately found himself besieged with demands for his Eindekkers with their synchronised guns. Pilots along the whole Front wanted to fly this amazing machine with its unrivalled power to destroy enemy machines in moments. A new version, the E11, was put into production but when Boelcke complained that the weight of the gun made the aeroplane unwieldy, Fokker quickly built a new machine and sent one to Boelcke, the other to Immelmann.

In the face of this new weapon – which, like all revolutionary inventions, made all other aircraft immediately redundant or obsolete – the British and French were helpless. They were lucky, at least to start with, as the Eindekkers were few in number and, for a while, the Fokker menace was more of a threat than an actuality. But as 1915 drew to a close, production of the new E111 model began to improve and Allied casualties began to mount.

So serious did the situation become that the RFC actually issued an order that any aircraft engaged in reconnaissance or artillery spotting had to be protected by no less than three fighters. It was merely a stop-gap answer as the British fighters of the time were invariably two-seater pusher aircraft and were no match for the fast Eindekkers. But it was something and it was certainly an acknowledgement of the problems the Front Line Squadrons of the RFC were facing.

The introduction of the V formation, where 'box fire' from the observers of the escorting machines offered at least a measure of protection, did go some way to curtailing the threat of the Fokkers. However, pilots like Immelmann with lightning fast reflexes and the ability to dive out of the sun, fire and zoom away almost before the enemy formation knew what was coming, meant that 1915–16 was a difficult time for Allied airmen.

Boelcke and Immelmann were the German star pilots, leaders of the pack and undoubtedly at the forefront in taking the aerial war to the Allies. Not

Death was a constant factor for all airmen, particularly during the Fokker Scourge of 1916. This shows the grave of French aviator Mendes.

everyone was convinced, however, either about the Eindekkers or the quality of men like Immelmann. James McCudden, now operating more and more as an observer, encountered the German ace at close quarters:

> By now the Fokker was trying to get behind us again, but my pilot was turning as quickly as the Fokker, whose pilot at last saw it was no good, and then went off to the east. As he drew away from us, I distinctly noticed that the pilot sat very high in his machine, and was wearing black flying kit - - - We were almost certain that the pilot of the Fokker was Immelmann and, if so, all I can say is that to my mind he would not fight even when the odds were even.[45]

The synchronised gun and the resultant success of the rampaging Fokkers were so significant that, for a while, German pilots were forbidden to cross the lines in case one of them should be brought down and the secret revealed. Of course, inevitably, this was exactly what happened but, by then, British and French designers were already working on their own versions of the interrupter gear.

A rudimentary version was introduced on Allied aircraft but it was not until March 1917 that George Constantinescu, a Romanian scientist, successfully designed and introduced a hydraulic machine gun synchroniser, using hydraulic oil pressure. This duly replaced the various types of mechanical interrupter gears then in service.

The Fokker Scourge reached its height in the spring of 1916, but this was probably as much to do with Boelcke's theories and tactics as it was with the superiority of German aircraft. By the end of 1915 only eighty-six of the new E111 Eindekkers had been built and put into service while, in opposition, there were nearly 230 Nieuports and DH2s, the only Allied aircraft capable of matching them. What the Allies lacked were pilots of the calibre of Boelcke and Immelmann and the publicity machine to make sure everyone knew about them.

Boelcke, the first real tactician of the aerial war, believed in large-scale fighter groups – the forerunners of the later Flying Circuses – which had three main tasks. Firstly they were to prevent enemy air activity. Then they were to defend and protect German reconnaissance planes. Lastly they were to attack ground forces.[46]

Whatever the reason, by the time the German assault on Verdun began at the end of February 1916, there was a very real risk of the Allied air forces being driven out of the sky. Such was the superiority of the German aircraft and pilots.

Some of the early German aces are shown on this postcard. Included are Boelcke (top centre) and Immelmann (top right). Germany quickly became aware of the propaganda value of her pilots and cards like this were eagerly bought by the German public – Boelcke and Immelmann became household names.

THE EARLY ACES

As the war in the air began to change from a gentlemanly wave to a deadly battle for survival, there came the emergence of a new phenomenon – the ace. The word 'ace' had been used in France before the war, indicating a sportsman who performed at a level high above others in his particular field. Soon it was being used to denote pilots who, by their superior skill and ability, had shot down a number of enemy aircraft.

The French first coined the idea, the honour being given to any pilot who had downed five or more aircraft. The first ace was, naturally enough, a Frenchman, Eugene Gilbert, who destroyed five German planes before he, too, was shot down and killed in the summer of 1915.

The early French aces were men who had already made names for themselves before the war. There was Roland Garros, of course, but his fame lasted only for a few brief weeks before he was forced down in enemy territory and the deflector blades, the secret of his success, was revealed.

After his capture Garros was incarcerated in a prisoner of war camp. He made a number of escape attempts before finally succeeding on 14 February 1918. He rejoined the French army and was posted to Escadrille No. 26. Flying a SPAD he gained two victories before he was shot down and killed on 5 October, one month before the end of the war and one day before his thirtieth birthday. Hermann Habich was credited with bringing him down.

Adolph Calestin Pegoud had already served in the French army before becoming a test pilot for Bleriot in 1913. He was renowned as the first man to

French pilot Adolph Calestin Pegoud sets off on a bombing mission, watched by a rather disinterested group of mechanics and soldiers. They have obviously seen it all before.

loop-the-loop although, in fact, Russian pilot Pyotr Nesterov had performed the manoeuvre a few days before – it was just that nobody knew about it! When war broke out in 1914, Pegoud was working as a flying instructor but immediately volunteered for combat and became an observation pilot.

On 5 February 1915 Pegoud and his observer shot down two German aircraft and forced another to land. Soon he was flying Morane-Saulnier Scouts and by July 1915 he had claimed his sixth victim. He was awarded the Croix de Guerre and lionised in the French press. On 31 August, however, Pegoud was shot down and killed by Unteroffizer Kandulst, a twenty-six-year-old German pilot who had been taught to fly, pre-war, by none other than Pegoud himself.

Another pre-war flyer to achieve 'ace' status was Jules Vedrines. He had led something of a charmed life in the heady pre-war days, crashing into the sea while trying to fly from Trouville to Le Havre and gaining the world air speed record of 108 mph in 1912. Like Garros, Vedrines fitted angle plates to the propeller of his Morane and succeeded in shooting down several enemy planes. Vedrines survived the war only to die in an air crash in 1919.

The Germans realised quite quickly that the exploits of their Fokker pilots could be turned to advantage, providing wonderful publicity, both at home and abroad. Unlike the French, however, the Germans insisted that a man had to shoot down ten enemy aircraft in order to be called an ace. They insisted on eye witness evidence of a victory as well as some more tangible proof – one of the reasons men like Richthofen regularly landed to search for souvenirs from his victims.[47]

Although Hauptmann Hugo Geyer and Oberleutenant Egbert Kuhn were the first German airmen to take a machine gun into action – managing to shoot

The Morane-Saulnier monoplane quickly became an efficient killing machine in the hands of men like Roland Garros – until he was forced to land in Germany and the secret of the deflector blades on his propeller was discovered. This shows French ace Jules Vedrines, who also had deflector blades fitted to his propeller, about to take-off on patrol in his Morane scout.

down a French Voisin on 28 April 1915 – the first of the German aces was Max Immelmann.

Immelmann was a rather cold and calculating Prussian who had trained himself to be a deadly shot – he once used no more than thirteen rounds to destroy a French two-seater. He developed a manoeuvre known as the Immelmann Turn. He would dive onto an enemy, firing, as he put it, when he was 'close enough to spit into the enemy's cockpit'. If the enemy plane did not fall, Immelmann would continue his dive past the enemy, and then zoom up in a loop. At the top of the loop he would half-roll, ready to attack again.

With his victory tally mounting by the day, Immelmann found himself the darling of German society. The Prussian was totally disinterested. All he wanted to do was shoot down French and British planes. He developed a close relationship with Anthony Fokker, regularly meeting with the Dutchman to decide on ways to improve his aircraft.

Then, on 18 June 1916 the German nation was sent into mourning when it was announced that Max Immelmann was dead. At first, desperate to preserve the myth of his invincibility, it was stated that mechanical failure had caused his plane to crash.

Tony Fokker would have none of it. He journeyed to the crash site, examined Immelmann's Eindekker and proved, beyond doubt, that there had been no accident. Immelmann had been killed in combat, shot down by Lieutenant G. S. McCubbin and Corporal J. H. Waller flying an FE2B in the skies over Annay.

Oswald Boelcke was the opposite of Immelmann, a happy and friendly man whose essential humanity sometimes persuaded him to bring gifts to wounded opponents in hospital. Yet in the air he was a deadly fighter who eventually had forty recorded victories against his name. He inspired other pilots by his quiet authority and by his willingness to listen to the opinions of anyone who had something valuable and sensible to say.

After the death of Max Immelmann, the German High Command became terrified that their only other air hero, Oswald Boelcke, would also be shot down and killed. Consequently, they withdrew him from combat duties, forbade him to fly and sent him on a series of inspection tours on the Western and Eastern Fronts.

It was during one of these tours, in Eastern Germany, that Boelcke first met the young and ambitious Manfred von Richthofen. When Boelcke finally managed to persuade the High Command to allow him back to the Front, it was with orders to form his own Jagdstaffel. Now he could choose the men to fly with him in what was, literally, a hunting pack with the avowed aim of driving Allied reconnaissance planes from the sky. Richthofen was one of the men Boelcke chose to join his Jasta.

The introduction of the Jagdstaffel concept was something Boelcke had been advocating for months. Despite the huge numbers of German planes in the sky during the Battle of Verdun, the French had been able to throw up even more

Max Immelmann poses beside one of his many victims. Distant and not really interested in fame, this is an unusual view of the German ace.

The first German ace, Immelmann was lionised by the press and by German High Command. This postcard shows him with the Kaiser and several high ranking German officers.

Fliegerhauptmann Boelcke ✝

Gefallen für das Vaterland,
Doch nicht gefällt von Feindeshand
Ist einer unfrer Besten.
Den Schrecken trugst du, deutscher Aar,
Hinein in unsrer Feinde Schaar
Im kampfdurchtobten Westen.

Du, der mit ungestümem Drang
Schon vierzig Feinde niederrang,
Du bist nun selbst gefallen.
Dein Name wird bewahret sein,
Viel besser als in Erz und Stein,
In unsern Herzen allen.

7776
Verlag von

W. Sanke

Oswald Boelcke was as charming as Immelmann was remote. Loved by the men of his Jasta, they and the whole of Germany were devastated when he was killed in an accidental collision high above the Western Front.

and by the time the battle stuttered to an end in the autumn of 1916 the French had wrested control of the air from the Germans, not because of quality pilots and aircraft but because of sheer numbers. The introduction of the Jagdstaffel, it was hoped, would soon be able to regain the lost advantage for Germany.[48]

For nearly a month Boelcke trained and instructed his young pilots before finally unleashing them on the unsuspecting Allies in September 1916. Richthofen and the others soon claimed their first kills.

On 28 October, Boelcke was leading his Jagdstaffel in an attack on two British aircraft when he was sent plunging to the ground after one of his young protégées came too close. The wheels of the young man's Albatross ripped off Boelcke's top wing and, as the pilots of the Jasta gazed on in helpless horror, their mentor fell to his death.

From the start, the RFC under Hugh Trenchard declared that it had no time for the 'ace' system. It would lead, Trenchard believed, to inappropriate comparisons between pilots and, in particular, would denigrate the excellent work of the two-seater reconnaissance and bombing planes whose work was as important as that of the more glamorous scout Squadrons.

For a long while the British fighter aces received virtually no publicity. Even as late as 1918, the name of Edward 'Mick' Mannock, arguably the greatest fighter pilot of the whole war, was unknown to the public. In any newspaper account of his activities, Mannock was referred to simply as 'Captain X'.

Despite this attitude, the names of some of the leading British pilots did eventually leak out and gradually became known, not just in the RFC but in public as well. One of the first to become famous was Major Lanoe George Hawker. Early in the war he had been active in bombing raids on places like Cologne and in the spring of 1915 he became the first man to shoot down two enemy aircraft (and sending a third fleeing for its life) in a single day. For this feat Hawker was awarded the Victoria Cross.

On 23 November 1916, Hawker became the eleventh victim of Manfred von Richthofen. It was a one-on-one fight that lasted for nearly twenty minutes, first one man gaining the upper hand, then the other. Around and around they circled, gradually losing height but always on the German side of the trenches. Hawker eventually had to break away to his own lines. His machine, a DH2 pusher, was outclassed by Richthofen's Albatross and the Red Baron was at last able to put a burst into Hawker's machine. The bullets caught the Englishman in the head. Hawker was buried with full military honours and Richthofen later dropped a note behind British lines, expressing his admiration for a brave and chivalrous opponent.[49]

Manfred von Richthofen (centre) with several of his pilots. Amongst the group are several other high scoring aces, notably Richthofen's brother Lothar (second from right) and Kurt Wolff (right).

Richthofen himself later wrote:

My eleventh Englishmen is Major Hawker, twenty six years old and commander of an English Squadron. Prisoners have said he was "the English Boelcke." It was the most difficult battle I have had but I finally shot him down.[50]

BOMBING, RECONNAISSANCE AND ARTILLERY SPOTTING

The fighter pilots of all nations, the exponents of a new kind of warfare, soon gained for themselves enviable reputations as carefree, daring champions of honourable combat. Yet their main purpose was always to defend the slower and more vulnerable reconnaissance and bombing aircraft. And while the work of these bomber and reconnaissance pilots was never going to be as glamorous as their fighter counterparts, they undoubtedly had their moments.

The first air VC of the war was won by a bomber pilot when, on 26 April 1915, Lieutenant William Rhodes-Moorhouse set out to attack Coutrai railway station, some 35 miles inside enemy lines. Armed with just a one-hundred pound-bomb, Rhodes-Moorhouse was subjected to heavy machine gun fire as soon as he approached the lines. His BE2 was hit and Rhodes-Moorhouse seriously wounded.

Despite his injuries, Rhodes-Moorhouse pressed on with his attack. Flying lower and lower as he approached his target, he reached Countai and dropped his bomb – the first low-level bombing attack ever made. The attack was successful but the pilot was hit again, mortally this time. He managed to limp back to his base at Merville but died of his wounds the following day. His posthumous VC was awarded in May 1915.

Reconnaissance of enemy positions was never an easy task. In 1915 reconnaissance came to mean taking photographs of enemy positions and that, in turn, meant flying in straight lines for protracted periods of time. The aircraft carrying out this job were incredibly vulnerable, not only to enemy fighters but also to Archie fired from the ground. One account of a reconnaissance mission, written by an anonymous British pilot, is worth quoting as it gives a clear indication of the danger involved in a routine but vital task:

As soon as I was in range the Germans opened on my machine, and then during the whole of the reconnaissance, which consisted of circling about a small area, they didn't give me a moment's peace. I had shells bursting round my machine the whole time, simultaneously flashes of flame and loud bangs, sometimes on one side and then on the other, below the machine,

William Rhodes-Moorehouse won the first aerial VC of the war when he bombed Coutrai Railway Station, 35 miles inside German lines. This drawing shows him high above the town but, in reality, he was forced lower and lower the closer he got to his destination.

Rhodes-Moorehouse was successful in his mission, damage to the station meaning that German troop movements were severely restricted for several days. He was mortally wounded but managed to return to his base and died a few hours later. His VC was awarded posthumously.

above it, behind it and in front, and some of them bumped the machine about unpleasantly. It was thoroughly uncomfortable.[51]

Pilots developed their skills and abilities in a desperate attempt to avoid the attention of Archie and enemy aircraft. It was unfortunate that the BE2, the main RFC reconnaissance plane, was inherently stable – a little less stability and a bit more unpredictability would have been welcome. It did not stop them trying:

> I twisted the machine about this way and that, made it side-slip outwards, and did everything I could to spoil their aim. But they kept me guessing the whole time. One shell exploded just in front, and I saw some bits of things flying off the engine and thought the propeller had gone.[52]

To begin with aerial photography was something that either worked or didn't. The technology for ensuring regular and lasting success simply did not exist. Observers carried cameras in their cockpits and simply leaned over the side of the plane in order to expose the plates. The obvious problem was that observers could not always guarantee to hold the camera level and so, after a while, cameras were attached to the outside of the fuselage by a means of leather straps.

An aerial photograph showing Observatory Ridge, a classic piece of reconnaissance and aerial photography. This was the type of photograph officers and men of the RFC and army had to try to decipher in order to make sense of the material brought back by the reconnaissance planes.

As the war progressed, better and more efficient cameras were introduced; the A type was succeeded, first, by the B and then by the C. The L type camera came into general use early in 1917. Unlike its predecessors, this was a semi-automatic camera with an adjustable lens and, importantly, it took its photographs through a hole in the floor of the fuselage.[53] Photographs were developed as soon as the reconnaissance machines returned to base, often on the aerodromes themselves, and quickly passed on to Headquarters.

Using photographs taken from the air, a complete picture was soon built up of the trench systems of both sides and men became expert at deciphering what they saw on the prints that were soon overflowing their desks. Accurate information was also compiled about the enemy rear areas, the complete infrastructure that supported the troops in the front line being mapped out and detailed.

Artillery was the major weapon of the war, killing far more men than machine guns and causing untold damage, both in the front lines and in rear areas. The traditional method of directing gunfire was for artillery units to use Forward Observation Posts, artillery officers taking up positions close to the trenches and reporting back on the fall of shot, on hits and misses, on new targets that had presented themselves and so on. They continued with this procedure until the end of the war. But it was a costly and dangerous business. The poet Edward Thomas was killed while undertaking exactly these duties at the Battle of Arras in the spring of 1917. He was only one of many.

A photographic section of the RFC at work, developing prints in a mobile unit on the aerodrome before sending them to Headquarters for interpretation. Developing and, even more importantly, interpreting the images brought back by the pilots – German, British and French – became one of the new arts brought out by the war.

A far more effective process was the use of aeroplanes as artillery spotters. Getting information back to the various units was the main problem. Early in the war, planes flashed signal lights or even fired flares but it was an amateur business, one that was easily misinterpreted or misunderstood.

The development of wireless telegraphy took artillery spotting to a new level. A message sent in Morse Code gave an instantaneous feedback to the gunners so that range and direction could be altered almost at will. Combined with the 'clock' system – 'Fire at twelve-o-clock, One-o-clock, etc.' – and the later zone calls where the Front was divided into a number of zones or specific areas, wireless telegraphy took the business of artillery spotting to a totally new level.

The early transmitters were very heavy and cumbersome, but in 1915 the introduction of the light Sterling Transmitter made the task much easier. It was also safer as the size of the early sets had precluded the presence of an observer or gunner – now observers were carried, providing better protection for the spotting aircraft.[54]

6

THE ZEPPELIN TERROR

For several years before the war began something of a 'Zeppelin Mania' had swept through Britain. It was part of a universal mass hysteria with dozens of books and articles being written about invasion plans and schemes, invariably far-fetched and fantastic plots hatched by the Kaiser and the wicked German Empire. Erskine Childers famous novel *Riddle of the Sands* was perhaps the best of them but there were many more – usually of very dubious pedigree.

Giant aerial armadas were a major part of the hysteria. Most people had never seen an airship, of course, and fear of the unknown is always greater than the commonplace. Over the years fear of sudden bombardment by Germany's enormous Zeppelin fleet grew to demonic dimensions and became a terror that was used to frighten children and adults alike.

The fact that Germany did not have the number of airships everyone supposed meant that there was no immediate aerial assault on Britain once war began. Indeed, in August 1914 the much vaunted Zeppelin fleet consisted of just twelve airships, two of these being already obsolete and seven others totally unsuitable for combat.[55] The rumours continued, of course. The most notable was that Roland Garros had crashed his aeroplane into a Zeppelin in order to save the town of Nancy from attack. It was a fanciful story but one that was believed for many years.

It was not until early in 1915 that Germany's much-vaunted fleet of airships finally came into operational existence. At first the Kaiser was reluctant to sanction raids on Britain. It would, after all, be breaching Article 25 of the Hague Convention of 1907 which had expressly forbidden aerial attacks on cities and centres of civilian population. In the end public pressure forced his hand and, somewhat reluctantly, Kaiser Wilhelm gave his approval for attacks to begin.

The first Zeppelin raid on Britain took place on 19 January 1915 when two navy airships flew over Great Yarmouth on the east coast and dropped a number of small bombs. Four people were killed, a number injured and some damage was caused to houses. It was a minor raid but, suddenly, all the long held fears of the British public became reality – the country could no longer boast of splendid isolation.

Between April and October that year nineteen airship attacks were launched against Britain; the first attack on London took place on 31 May. The Zeppelin,

THE RAIDER
PUBLICATION SANCTIONED BY OFFICIAL PRESS BUREAU.
PUBLISHING OFFICE:
39, ST. ANDREW'S HILL, E.C.
(Copyright)

The fear engendered by Zeppelin raids spread throughout Britain. The fact that the raiders came by night simply added to the terror.

LZ-38, involved in that London raid was commanded by Hauptmann Erich Linnarz, who had, earlier in the month, also bombed Southend.

During that earlier flight Linnarz had thrown a suitably demonic message from the gondola of his airship: 'You English. We have come and will come again soon. Kill or cure. German.'[56] It was a curious, not to say inflammatory, message, one that not only shows the attitudes of the Zeppelin crews but also indicates that they were well aware of the fear induced by the giant airships on the civilians below.

On the night of 17 May, Linnarz and his airship had a lucky escape when Flight Lieutenant Bigsworth became the first man to engage a Zeppelin in aerial combat. Tracking the airship back to its base, over Ostend, he dropped four 20-lb bombs onto LZ-38. They exploded on the fabric of the Zeppelin and one crewman died. The airship limped home with its starboard propeller dead and a huge gash in the fabric of its gas bag.

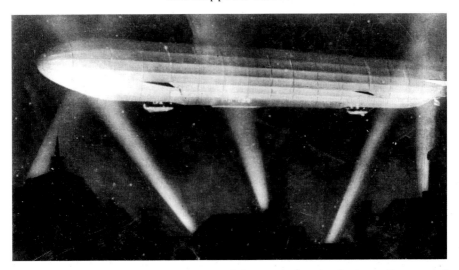

British defences were slow to develop and for many months the Zeppelins seemed invulnerable, attacking wherever and whenever they liked.

The 31 May attack on London was a significant raid. Thirty explosive bombs and over ninety incendiaries were dropped, the target area ranging from Stepney to Leytonstone. Seven civilians were killed and damage of somewhere in the region of £18,000 was caused.[57] The following night another raid took place, this time killing over twenty people.

It was not just London and the south of England that suffered. In the spring of 1915 raids were also launched against coastal shipping and on ports in East Anglia. In April, LZ-9 under Kapitanleutnant Heinrich Mathy, perhaps the most famous and daring of all the Zeppelin commanders, carried out a raid on the north-east coast of the country, bombs dropping on Wallsend and Humberside. The material effect of these raids was minimal but fear of death from the air remained constant.

Now, with hindsight, it is hard to understand quite why the Zeppelin raids caused so much fear and such widespread terror. The airships were singularly ill-suited for combat, being unwieldy and always at risk to the vagaries of the weather. The higher they flew, the less effective they became. Their bomb load was minimal and despite being well armed and defended, their very size made them relatively easy targets. They were dangerous all right but, with their explosive gasses, probably far more dangerous to the crewmen on board than they were to the civilian and military targets below.

However, like all mass hysteria, the fear was irrational. It was the image, the thought of these giant machines nosing through a low cloud base, running almost silently towards their target, which set people's nerves on edge. And for those few months in 1915 and early 1916 their mystique and power gripped the whole of Britain.

This German drawing of the forward compartment of a Zeppelin as originally published in *Illustrierte Zeitung*. The view shows the Zeppelin commander studying a map and a crewman climbing the ladder to the outside of the airship. It all seems rather spacious and well-ordered – literary and artistic licence for the benefit of the German public.

FIGHTING THE MENACE

Faced by the prospect of Zeppelins causing major damage, both to the industrial regions of Britain and to the residential areas of cities like London, the government appointed Sir Percy Scott to take charge of the capital city's defences.

Scott knew that aircraft could – and, eventually, would – be the way to combat the Zeppelin menace. But as the airships invariably attacked at night, first the pilots would have to learn the tricky business of night flying. In the meantime, London's anti-aircraft defences would have to be strengthened.

While members of the Royal Naval Air Service carried out bombing attacks on the Zeppelin bases – with varying degrees of success – Scott promptly threw away all the pom-pom guns currently in use, declaring that they were worse than useless. A French 75-mm field gun was introduced instead, mounted on the back of a lorry to enable it to be driven across London to wherever danger threatened. In time, this weapon was augmented by six high-angle Vickers guns and a number of searchlights. A light cruiser was also moored in the Thames, equipped with high-angle guns, but she – like most of the anti-aircraft weapons – did more for civilian morale than cause any real threat to the airships.

Bomb damage on the morning after a Zeppelin raid.

The aft compartment of an attacking Zeppelin, complete with mechanics working on the engines and gunners keeping a sharp look out for enemy fighters. This, you feel, is a realistic depiction of what it must have been like on board one of the raiders.

Early attempts to destroy the raiders were woefully inadequate. Aircraft were sent up to intercept, time after time. Mostly they failed to locate the Zeppelins and when they did encounter one their gunfire or bombs – popular wisdom of the time declared that dropping bombs on them was the only way to bring down an airship – had little effect. It was hard enough to spot the airships at night, let alone destroy them!

In February 1916, at a joint Admiralty and War Office Conference, it was formally agreed that it would be the task of the RNAS to try to prevent Zeppelins from reaching Britain; the RFC would be responsible for destroying those that did manage to get through. It was the start of a slow but sure build-up, an effective system of defending the shores of Britain.

By the beginning of 1917 there were eleven Home Defence Squadrons in position, most of them on the east and south coast, under the command of Lieutenant General T. C. R. Higgins. Of these, Squadrons 37, 39, 50 and 78 had particular responsibility for the defence of London. They each had a headquarters airfield, linked by telephone to various Warning Centres, and a number of satellite aerodromes.[58]

The creation of this Home Defence Wing did take some forty or fifty aircraft away from the Western Front – something the German High Command had been banking on – but equipping them with the latest incendiary ammunition did at least give the aeroplanes a chance of bringing down a Zeppelin or two.

BRINGING DOWN THE BEAST

In fact the first aerial victory over a Zeppelin had already occurred many months before, not above the green fields of Britain but close to the Front in Belgium. It occured on 7 June 1915.

Flying a Morane-Saulnier Type L monoplane, Flight Sub Lieutenant Reginald Warneford of the RNAS located LZ-37 over Ostend as she returned from a mission. He chased the Zeppelin towards Ghent and climbing to 11,000 feet, he positioned himself above the airship. From there he dropped six 20-lb bombs onto the giant machine. They struck their target and exploded; the blast was so violent that Warneford's plane was blown onto its back and the engine stopped.

The Zeppelin fell in a ball of flame, smashing into the ground and spreading its remains over a wide area. Unfortunately, some of the debris fell on a convent. Two of the sisters were killed but one crewman from the Zeppelin, the only survivor, smashed through the nunnery roof and, with incredible luck, landed on a bed – the only soft surface in the nunnery. Warneford managed to regain control of his plane and put her down behind German lines. He took 35 minutes to repair his engine before taking off and returning to his base and a rapturous welcome.

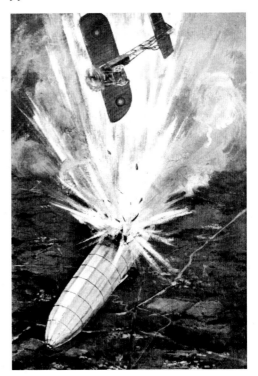

Warneford gets his Zeppelin. Attacking LZ-37 over Ghent, Flight Sub-Lieutenant Reginald Warneford of the RNAS became the first pilot to bring down a Zeppelin when he dropped six bombs onto the top of the airship. His Morane-Saulnier scout was turned upside down by the explosion and he was lucky to make an emergency landing behind enemy lines.

Within twenty-four hours Warneford had been awarded the Victoria Cross, only the second airman to be so honoured. He was informed of the decoration in a telegram from the King:

> I most heartily congratulate you upon your splendid achievement of yesterday, in which you, single-handed, destroyed an enemy Zeppelin. I have much pleasure in conferring upon you the Victoria Cross for this gallant act – George, RI.

Never before had a VC been awarded so quickly after the event, and never before had the recipient been informed of the award by the reigning sovereign. It was not a bad return for the young pilot, about whom his flying instructor once said that he would either do big things or kill himself!

In the event, Warneford did both. A fortnight after his success he received the Legion d'honneur from the French government, being presented with the medal by none other than General Joffre himself.

Then, after a celebratory lunch, Warneford took an American journalist, Henry Beach Newman, up for a flight in a new Henri Farman. At 200 feet the right wing collapsed and both Warneford and Newman, neither of whom was wearing a seat belt, were thrown from the plane. Newman was killed instantly and Warneford died on his way to hospital.[59]

Just two weeks after his success, Warneford – now the proud holder of the Victoria Cross – was killed in a flying accident. This 'In Memorium' card was published shortly afterwards.

MORE SUCCESS

The first airship to be brought down over British soil was not actually a Zeppelin but the wooden framed Schutte-Lanz SL-11. As far as the public was concerned, the difference was a mere technicality. It was a victory over the German terror weapon.

On the night of 2/3 September 1916, flying a BE2c and with his guns loaded with incendiary bullets, Lieutenant William Leefe Robinson, flying from his base, Sutton's Farm near Hornchurch, spotted the enemy airship over Essex. SL-11 was one of sixteen airships despatched to bomb London that night. In the event high wind and rain scattered the Zeppelin fleet and only one of them managed to reach the target. When SL-11 was caught in the beam of a searchlight over Essex, it was pure luck that Leefe Robinson was close by.

Firing from beneath the airship, Leefe Robinson emptied a drum of incendiary ammunition into its belly. There was no effect. Leefe Robinson then climbed above the airship and fired again. This time a thin trickle of flame emerged from the side of the raider and then SL-11 exploded in a mass of fire and smoke. The airship commander, Wilhelm Schramm, and his fifteen strong crew all perished in the crash.

Thousands watched, cheering and screaming, as the stricken airship fell at Cuffley near Enfield. Three days later Leefe Robinson was awarded the Victoria Cross but, more importantly, he immediately became a hero in the eyes of the British public. Postcards of the wrecked airship and the pilot were published and sold in their thousands. Robinson was sent presents and telegrams, even a cheque for £2,000 from the city of Newcastle.

The RFC might not have agreed with the idea of lionising its aces but, such was the power of public opinion, they certainly made an exception in the case of Leefe Robinson. Public adoration soared and he could, literally, not walk down the road without being accosted by young girls. Leefe Robinson was seen as the man who, single-handedly, had saved the nation from a terrible fate. Of course, it could not last but while it did the stock of the Royal Flying Corps was never greater.

In fact, the destruction of SL-11 created something of a watershed in the fight against the raiding airships. Within a few weeks L-32 was brought down by Lieutenant Frederick Sowrey. Watched by thousands of eager spectators, the Zeppelin crashed and burned at Billericay in Essex.

On the night of 1 October, Lieutenant Wulstan Tempest caught up with L-31, piloted by Heinrich Mathy, over Potters Bar. Firing from below, Tempest

William Leefe Robinson became the first man to destroy an airship over British soil when he attacked the wooden-framed Schutte-Lanz SL-11 (not, technically, a Zeppelin) on the night of 2/3 September 1916. Overnight, Leefe Robinson became a national hero.

poured two drums of ammunition into the Zeppelin's belly. He saw the airship begin to glow and 'go red inside like an enormous Chinese lantern'. It then dropped like a stone, narrowly missing Tempest and his aircraft, and crashed in a field outside the town. Heinrich Mathy, the most famous of all Zeppelin commanders, died along with his crew. His death caused widespread mourning in Germany, the outpouring of grief being similar to that which met the news of Immelmann's demise.[60]

In the weeks ahead, further victories by Lieutnants de Brandon, Saundby and Watkins clearly proved to the British public that the Zeppelins were not the invincible terror weapons that they had feared. They could be shot down.

GOD BLEW AND THEY WERE SCATTERED

In the end, however, it was the elements rather than the skill or bravery of British pilots that caused the defeat of the Zeppelins. They had already proved vulnerable to the effects of high winds.

Five naval Zeppelins had set out to bomb London on 16 March 1916, but a 40-mph wind forced them to abandon their mission. L-39 was blown across French lines where it was destroyed by anti-aircraft fire. In the face of these losses the German High Command cut back – although it did not suspend – its aerial attacks on Britain.

The night of 20 October 1916 saw the greatest Zeppelin disaster of the campaign when four airships, part of an eleven strong raiding force, were destroyed in a gale.

The end of one of these Zeppelins was particularly poignant. L-50 was driven back over the Channel by the wind and, around about midday on 21 October, tried to put down close to the trenches in Northern France. Fired on by the British artillery batteries she lumbered once more into the air, losing her forward gondola and its crew when she clipped the top of a nearby wood.

Driven before the wind, L-50 was soon over the southern coast of France. Pursued by French pilots, she passed on over the Mediterranean and was never seen again, presumably meeting her end somewhere over the empty vastness of the sea.

The raids had begun in a flurry of fear; they ended in abject failure. Ultimately, they were more of a nuisance value than anything else for although fifty-one raids were launched, the Zeppelins caused barely 500 casualties. And before the raids were suspended at the end of 1916, over fifty Zeppelins had been lost.[61]

As British defences, both aerial and anti-aircraft gunnery, improved so the Zeppelins were forced to fly higher and higher. This meant, of course, that bombing – with the relatively primitive bomb sights then available – became increasingly difficult. And, significantly, the greater the height at which they flew, the greater the effect of the weather on the airships.

Zeppelin killers! More success quickly followed Leefe Robinson's victory. This postcard view shows Leefe Robinson along with Wulstan Tempest and Frederick Sowrey, both of whom brought down airships within the month. By now, however, destruction of airships had become too commonplace and, instead of the VC, Tempest and Sowrey were awarded just a DSO each.

The wreckage of LZ-77, brought down by French anti-aircraft fire rather than the machine gun fire and bombs of British aircraft.

It was a long and dangerous trip from Belgium or France to the skies above London and, once the British defences became more organised, many airships were lost on the return journey.

The Zeppelin attacks might be over but raids on the British mainland soon took on a more serious dimension as fixed wing aircraft, in the shape of huge Gotha bombers, began to appear in the skies above London. For the moment, though, victory over the Zeppelins was enough.

Zeppelins were still commissioned and operated in Germany, almost to the end of the war. In all, approximately 112 Zeppelins were built between 1914 and 1918, many of them being used for reconnaissance and scouting. The 'Super Zeppelins' were introduced in 1916, machines that were equipped with six engines and a modified hull construction. In November 1917 one of these machines attempted to supply units fighting in German East Africa (an impossible task as the German Army had recently surrendered) and flew 4,000 miles before returning to base after a record-breaking flight. Graf von Zeppelin, inventor and presiding genius of the Zeppelin world, did not live to see such a feat as he had died on 8 March 1917.

BRITISH AIRSHIPS

Seven months before the war began, on 1 January 1914, all British airships became the responsibility of the Admiralty. Machines such as the Willows IV, the brain child of Cardiff balloon expert Ernest Willows – a private concern – and the Royal Aircraft Factory airships Delta, Eta and Gamma, were dutifully handed over.[62]

Ernest Willows and other private designers did not lose out. The Admiralty gave Willows a cheque for £1,000 for his airship, a huge sum that he promptly invested in spherical balloons, machines that did not interest the authorities. From January 1914 onwards, however, the 'senior service' took responsibility for the operation (and all future development) of British airships.

The Admiralty, considerably more insightful than the Army, had grasped the simple fact that airships could play a very useful role in defending the sea lanes, particularly by operations above the narrow English Channel, in the North Sea and out in the Western Approaches. They were to operate alongside seaplanes, spotting submarines and even, on occasion, attacking them.

Production quickly began on a fleet of coastal defence airships. To begin with standard aeroplane fuselages, usually from BE2 machines, were slung beneath the envelopes of the balloons, acting as gondolas or compartments for the crew. Almost 150 of these simple but effective airships were built and operated during the war, all of varying size. The later types were intended to cruise at up to 40 mph and have an endurance of between 16 and 18 hours.[63]

In order to maintain and supply such machines, a series of seaplane and airship stations soon sprang up around the coast. As long as the area chosen was sheltered with a good stretch of open water, these bases – although invariably of a temporary nature – provided a useful service for these coastal defence machines.

Operated by the RNAS, the pilots of the airships and seaplanes flew long hours over seemingly endless stretches of water, desperately attempting to spot the telltale wake of submarines on the surface. Sightings of U-boats were rare, attacks even rarer, but the sudden appearance of an airship or seaplane invariably forced the submarines to dive and, for a while at least, therefore rendered them almost ineffective.

'NULLI SECUNDUS' THE BRITISH ARMY AIRSHIP.

Nulli Secundus, an early army airship during an air display at Aldershot.

An early naval dirigible employed in the hunt for U-boats in the English Channel, North Sea and Western Approaches. The fuselage of a BE type aircraft was used as a cupola for the crew – open to the elements and bitterly cold when flying over miles of empty ocean.

An artist's impression of an airship on patrol protecting a convoy as it passes down the English Channel.

Airship development was sure and steady during the war years but the performance of the Coastal Class of airship, introduced in 1917, was nothing short of spectacular. One machine of this class flew more than 66,000 miles over a two year period, engaged in constant anti-submarine patrols around the British coast. By this time gondolas were enclosed and the airships even carried fixed machine guns on top of the envelope.

British airships clearly had a different purpose from the giant Zeppelins but they were immensely effective – far more effective than the Zeppelins. Theirs was an unglamorous war but one that, as hostilities continued and the German submarine threat intensified, became more and more necessary.

SEAPLANES

Seaplanes operated in conjunction with the airships and with the early surface escort vessels in an attempt to protect convoys of merchant ships and keep the sea lanes – on which Britain relied for food – well and truly open.

They could drop bombs or torpedoes, provided they were able to spot the enemy U-boats in the first place. Like the patrolling airships, their pilots were quite content to force enemy submarines to dive, thus preventing them from recharging the batteries for their electric motors. Any 'kill' was a decided bonus.

As early as 1915 the Admiralty had introduced the Short 225 Seaplane. Although it was predominantly an anti-submarine aircraft, it does have the distinction of being the only aeroplane to take part in the Battle of Jutland in 1916 when it was used for fleet reconnaissance duties. A plane of this type also managed to successfully torpedo a large Turkish transport ship during the Gallipoli campaign of 1915.[64]

Other seaplanes in use by the RNAS included the Sopwith Baby (effectively a Sopwith Pup with floats) and the Fairey Hamble. The great advantage of seaplanes over airships was that they were not quite so susceptible to the elements. As long as the water was calm enough for them to take-off and land, they could operate.

And, like the airships, some of the patrols they undertook were of immense duration. Taking just one Naval Air Station as an example, in April 1918 flying boats from RNAS Fishguard in west Wales flew thirty-one patrols, a total of 51 hours and 43 minutes. A distance of 3,460 miles was covered and only two patrols were aborted due to bad weather. In the week ending 29 June 1918, the same Squadron from Fishguard flew a total of twenty-nine patrols, lasting for 83 hours and 10 minutes. In that week alone 4,956 miles were covered – but only one possible contact was made with a U-boat.[65]

Clearly, the work was hard, exacting and, for the most part, unproductive. The boredom of endless hours spent patrolling over empty grey sea was

A Short Seaplane coming in to land. Note the wide open but calm waters of the estuary, an essential element if seaplanes were to work efficiently.

Seaplanes, like airships, were used to protect convoys and to spot enemy submarines. They made long and often fruitless patrols over oceans that would quickly swallow them up should they have to ditch or land.

a far cry from the hectic excitement of life on the Western Front. Flying such long and monotonous missions it was inevitable that accidents would happen and RNAS Fishguard, like many of its counterparts, suffered casualties.

On 21 February 1918 Flight Sub-Lieutenant Cyril Duckworth failed to return from patrol. His aircraft, a Fairey Hamble, was spotted, floating off Cardigan Island, several miles north of the base. The lifeboat from nearby St Dogmaels was launched and although the aircraft was recovered there was no sign of Duckworth. Exhausted and disorientated, he must have slipped into the sea and drowned – just one small tragedy but an occupational hazard for the men flying in defence of the British coast and sea lanes.[66]

OBSERVATION BALLOONS

The need to know the movements of enemy forces remained constant throughout the war. And one of the most effective ways of gathering such information was by the use of observation balloons.

These balloons were situated a mile or so behind the lines. Moored to the ground by wire, they were capable of rising to altitudes of at least 3000 feet, from which vantage point they had a wonderful view of the enemy trenches and rear areas. To begin with the balloons were raised or brought down by

OBSERVATION BALLOON OFF TO WATCH THE ENEMY.

An observation balloon being hoisted into the sky over France. Observers in the balloons carried out an unheralded but essential task, keeping watch on enemy positions and troop movements.

British soldiers haul down an observation balloon, a hard and thankless task
– particularly if enemy planes were attacking. In later years motor winches replaced
the hand operation.

Balloon observers were
given parachutes – unlike
their counterparts in
aircraft. They were
not always effective,
however, and many
observers jumped, not to
safety but to their deaths.
This shows a German
observer leaping from
the basket of his balloon,
using a standard issue
Paulus parachute.

hand-operated winches but from the summer of 1915 motor driven winches were used to increase the speed of operation.

Balloons were a crucial part of the artillery infrastructure and, therefore, they were always well defended. Anti-aircraft guns, flaming onions and lurking squadrons of fighters were all used to defend these vital pieces of equipment. Pilots believed the flaming onions to be balls of liquid fire, joined together by wire, rather like a South American bolas. In fact, they were just tracer rounds fired by a five-barrelled mortar and the idea that they were linked together was no more than an optical illusion. It did not stop them being a terrifying ordeal, as Canadian ace Billy Bishop outlined:

> The onions are shot upward from some kind of mortar. The first thing you see is a big cluster of six or eight whirling balls of fire coming at you from below - - - They all rotate rapidly, giving off flames so that each of the balls seems to have a potential diameter of five or six feet of flame.[67]

Most airmen soon realised that attacking balloons was a quick way to the grave but some, men like the German Heinrich Gontermann, the American Frank Luke and the Belgian Willie Coppens, specialised in shooting them down.

The need to defend observation balloons was hammered home to all fighter pilots. Camel pilot Roy Crowden wrote about one such attempt:

> Fourteen Huns came down on our balloons. Unfortunately they got two before we could get to them. But myself and Green, a chap in my Flight, a South African, stopped them. I shot one fat Albatross down. He hit Kennel Hill but I couldn't get him confirmed officially as it was rather misty and 'Archie' couldn't see. Still, I'm sure I got him and that's all that matters.[68]

Pilots did not use parachutes at this time. They were in existence but the RFC refused to issue them, believing that, if they were given out, a man in charge of a damaged aircraft would happily jump out, rather than try to bring his machine home. The German Air Force did issue Paulus parachute equipment to some of their pilots and the ace Ernst Udet once used one to escape from his burning aircraft. In contrast, balloon observers on both sides, men who had little or no control over their machines, were all given parachutes.

The parachutes were not always effective, however. When five German balloons were shot down by French fighters using incendiary rockets during the Battle of Verdun, all the observers dutifully and uniformly leapt from their baskets. None of the parachutes opened and all of the men were killed, although whether this was due to equipment failure or operator error will never be known.[69]

7

DAWN PATROL

Imagine the scene. Pilots sit in their cockpits, engines idling, as far away in the eastern sky the first splinters of light begin to punch holes into the blackness of night. Breakfast – invariably hard boiled eggs – has been taken and now the smell of burning oil and the hum of aero engines fill the air. A sense of urgency and expectation lies across the airfield.

Finally the signal is given – a wave of the hand, a Very Light, a flash with a torch, whatever device is chosen – and, one after the other, the pilots and the aeroplanes follow the flight commander down the grass runway and up into the sky. The Dawn Patrol has begun.

Air mechanics stare after the departing aircraft, wondering if any or all of the planes they so lovingly care for will make it back to the aerodrome in a few hours time. They watch the eastern sky for a while, eyes trained on the receding dots, then turn away to other duties.

If the scene appears to be something of a cliché then that's probably because it is, but a cliché is only a truism that has become a household phrase and the description is valid because it is so true.

Regular patrols above the trenches were routine for the pilots of all fighter aircraft. Dawn Patrol went up at first light, followed by a succession of further incursions until night fell and flying was no longer possible. Sometimes there was a Squadron 'show' when all of the aircraft went up together but patrols of between three and five aircraft were the usual fighter force.

Experienced flight commanders would use the elements – a low cloud base or a position high up 'in the sun' – in order to trap unwary enemy aircraft and the aim of all fighter pilots was to clear the sky of reconnaissance aircraft. Dogfights against enemy fighters did happen but the primary purpose of all fighters was to shoot down opposition two-seaters. That was why they were there; that was why they flew their regular patrols.

OFFENSIVE V. DEFENSIVE

Almost from the beginning of aerial warfare, pilots on both sides of the lines were faced with a huge dilemma – whether to fight a defensive or offensive war.

Immelmann and Boelcke had both favoured an offensive campaign, using the superiority of their Fokker Eindekkers to sweep the enemy reconnaissance planes out of the sky. It suited their temperaments and the tactics they developed.

However, by the beginning of the Battle of the Somme in July 1916 the Allies had achieved a clear numerical superiority in the air. It was a position they were not to lose for the rest of the war. And it was this very superiority of numbers that led the Germans to adopt a defensive campaign.

The British tried to protect their slower reconnaissance planes by establishing a protective barrier of fighters between the enemy and the Front Line – in other words they would take the war into German territory. What this meant was that the German Jagdstaffeln could simply wait, high up in the sun, as the British approached and then dive on the enemy when they were well beyond their own lines.

While this was a potentially dangerous tactic, it was also a situation that appealed to many of the red-blooded RFC pilots. It meant that even an experienced flight commander like James McCudden had a hard time of it, keeping some of his wilder charges in control:

> We went down on these Huns a long way east of the Menin-Roulers Road. I had a very anxious time firing recall signals for the benefit of Barlow and Rhys-Davids, who would have chased the Huns over to the Russian front if I had let them.[70]

An added problem for both British and French pilots – although the French, like the Germans, tended to stay on their own side of the lines – was that

RFC graves somewhere in France, old propellers serving as headstones.

the prevailing wind on the Western Front was westerly. It meant that German aircraft had the wind behind them as they turned for home while the RFC machines were always battling into the wind as they tried to get back to base.

And sometimes, limping back, low on fuel and just a few hundred feet above the trenches, British aircraft were in as much danger from their own gunners as they were from the Germans:

> I'm ashamed to say that we usually fired at anything that flew overhead, especially if it was low down and we felt we might just hit it. We'd blaze away, with rifles and machine guns, and never give a thought to the nationality of the plane or the pilot. It was instinctive – the aeroplane was up there and we were going to have a pot at it. It was a bit like throwing stones at birds. Thank God we never hit anything![71]

Sir Hugh Trenchard was convinced that only offensive action in the air could possibly help British infantry to follow a similar pattern on the ground. Trenchard's view and, therefore, his order was that the RFC should take the war to the Germans – and they should do it regardless of the cost. It undoubtedly meant the death of many young airmen but it fostered the offensive spirit in the RFC and created a tradition that lasted right the way through to the Second World War.

Trenchard's policy came to fruition at the Battle of the Somme as British fighters ranged, almost unchallenged, over the battlefield.

Two British airmen, shot down in combat, are marched into captivity by German soldiers. One of them, at least, looks to be badly shaken up and has to be assisted away.

And it was not just the fighters. Bombers were ordered to concentrate themselves into large formations and attack only significant targets. Raids on targets within 30 miles of the front lines were to be escorted by fighters – anything more distant and one in five of the bombers would carry no bombs but equip themselves with extra gunners in order to offer protection to the bombing formation.[72] It was a tactic that was not always successful but it certainly showed Trenchard's intentions.

PLANES AND PLANES AND...

The story of aerial warfare between 1914 and 1918 is one of new or revolutionary development followed by even newer counter-development as one side gained the upper hand, then the other.

Arguably, it all began when Roland Garros fitted deflector wedges to his propeller blades and, for a few short weeks, reigned supreme in the skies over France. When he was brought down behind enemy lines and captured, the German High Command decided that they, too, needed an aeroplane that fired forward through the propeller. The result was Anthony Fokker's Eindekker E1, a machine that gained absolute supremacy for the German Army Air Service.

The RFC responded with the DH2 single-seater scout and the FE2b two-seater. These aircraft appeared above France in the first part of 1916 and over the next few months wrested control of the skies from the Fokker Eindekkers. They were pusher aircraft, however, the propeller being set behind the pilot, and with rapid developments being made in terms of effective interrupter gear, it was clear that their active life as front line fighter aircraft was going to be limited.

The DH2 made up the first homogeneous RFC Squadron, with all of the aircraft being of the same type. This was No. 24 Squadron under the command of the redoubtable Major Lanoe Hawker and the immediate success of the Squadron ensured that it was a process that would soon be repeated throughout the RFC.

The DH2 and FE2b machines were largely responsible for the British command of the skies during the Battle of the Somme, but their period of ascendancy was over almost before it began.

The German response came towards the end of the Somme battle, in the autumn of 1916, when they introduced the Halberstadt and Albatross D1 and D11 Scouts. These sleek, fast fighting machines quickly regained aerial superiority for Germany, totally outclassing the slower, more ponderous British pushers. The only aircraft capable of matching them were the British Sopwith Pup and the French SPAD, but as these new Allied planes were still not available in great numbers they could not prevent German ascendancy.[73]

Although introduced onto the Western Front in early 1917, the two-seater Bristol Fighter was not the immediate success that Trenchard and the High

The FE2b two-seater, one of the pusher aircraft that wrested control of the skies from the Germans and ended the Fokker Scourge.

The German Army Air Service introduced the Halberstadt Scout in the summer of 1916. It was the first German biplane to be fitted with interrupter gear and a forward firing machine gun.

3668

The first Albatross scout, the DI, came into service in September 1916. This view shows the later DIII, one of the most effective fighter planes of the war. The V struts on the wing made the machine immediately recognisable to Allied pilots.

Command had hoped for. Mistakenly used in the tight V formation employed by most two-seaters, a formation that did not allow it the freedom to use both forward and rear firing guns, the first combat flight on 5 April – led by Leefe Robinson of Zeppelin fame – was decimated by von Richthofen's Jasta.

Four of the six Bristol Fighters from No. 43 Squadron were shot down, another severely damaged. Leefe Robinson was brought down behind enemy lines and taken prisoner where his fame as a VC winner and as the victor over SL-11 ensured that he was given a hard time in the POW camp. Despite many escape attempts he remained in custody until the end of the war, only to die in the subsequent Spanish flu epidemic.

Despite its false start the Bristol Fighter – once pilots worked out how to use it – became one of the most successful aeroplanes of the whole war. It was particularly effective at high altitude and remained in service with RAF units until 1931.

Once the SPAD Scouts could be produced in quantity they were instrumental in, yet again, wresting aerial control from the Germans. Used principally by French forces – only two RFC Squadrons were equipped with them – the machine was also used by the American air arm once the USA entered the war in 1917.

Perhaps the most famous of all British fighters were introduced in the spring and summer of 1917, the SE5a and the Sopwith Camel. They have been called, respectively, the Hurricane and Spitfire of the First World War, an invidious comparison that does not begin to take account of the stable gun platform provided by the SE5 or the idiosyncrasies of the Camel that made it one of the

Despite a disastrous introduction during the Battle of Arras in 1917, the two-seater Bristol Fighter was one of the best Allied aircraft to operate during the war, being particularly effective for long range and high altitude work. By 1918 over 1,700 'Brisfits' were being used by the RAF and the plane continued in use for many years afterwards.

most effective fighter aircraft of the war. The Camel remained in service until the end of 1918, accounting for 980 enemy aircraft.[74]

The German response came in a modified and improved Albatross, the D111, and the famous Fokker Triplane. The Triplane was first used in August 1917; Werner Voss shot down twenty-one British aircraft in as many days, although there is a school of thought that says Voss owed his success to British pilots mistaking his Fokker for the Sopwith Triplane which was already well used by the RNAS. With its three wings, the Fokker Triplane had an amazing rate of climb and in the hands of men like Voss and von Richthofen it was very manoeuvrable.

Richthofen became devoted to the machine and persuaded Anthony Fokker to make him a specially strengthened and modified version. However, despite the success of Richthofen and his Jasta, the Triplane did not quite manage to steal control of the air from the SPADs, SE5s and Camels. New fighter machines were required.

Anthony Fokker immediately came up with what was probably Germany's best machine of the war, the Fokker D.V11. The plane had a fuselage made of tubular steel, covered with canvas, and was particularly effective at heights where Allied aircraft were sluggish to handle. Unfortunately, by the time it was introduced in the early summer of 1918, the tide of war had turned against Germany and the D.V11 was unable to influence the outcome of the conflict.

The Sopwith Snipe was a development of the Sopwith Camel but it was in use for only a few months before the Armistice was signed in November 1918.

The SE5a was the favourite machine of the great 'Hun getters'. It was such a stable gun platform that men like McCudden and Mannock notched up huge victory scores in the aircraft.

The one aeroplane that everybody recognises from the Great War is the Sopwith Camel. They were not easy to fly but were very easy to crash, particularly on landing – as this view of a Camel sitting on its nose clearly shows.

The Fokker Triplane, a plane that climbed like the devil but which had a tendency to shed its wings when diving steeply. It was the favourite aircraft of German aces like Manfred von Richthofen and Werner Voss.

The Sopwith Snipe came into service in 1918 and was probably the finest Allied aircraft of the war. Unfortunately for the British airmen it was never delivered in high enough quantities to make a significant difference to the war in the air.

The Snipe represented the culmination of fighter development during the war years and while only 250 of them went into service on the Western Front, the machine remained in use with the RAF for many years after the war.

There were dozens of other planes used by all sides in the war. For Germany the AEG C1V was developed specifically for ground attacks and was fitted with armour plating to protect the pilot and observer. Highly successful in this role, it was called 'The Flying Tank' by British airmen. For Britain, machines like the Sopwith Dolphin where the pilot sat with his head above the backward staggered upper wing and the DH9 with its fuel tanks directly below the cockpit, were not popular but did their jobs efficiently and effectively.

AERODROME ATTACKS

As the value of aircraft as a weapon of war became fully appreciated, so too did the need to destroy them. And if they could not be shot down in aerial combat, the next best way was to destroy them on the ground. Most aerodromes were fifteen to twenty miles behind the front lines, far enough away to be safe from artillery and infantry attacks but well within range of marauding aircraft.

With this end in mind attacks on enemy aerodromes soon became a regular occurrence. Often these were bombing attacks from fairly high altitude but

This aerial view of an Allied airfield in the Verdun sector, complete with hangars and aircraft lined up in front, shows what an excellent target such places made for enemy flyers.

sometimes they consisted of lightning raids by fighters using rockets, small bombs and machine guns. Anti-aircraft and machine guns were used to try to shoot down the raiders, most aerodromes being well defended. And sometimes their efforts were successful:

> The Huns came over, very low, and dropped bombs on our 'drome. We hit one Hun with machine gun fire and our AA fire got one Hun in flames.[75]

Anti-aircraft defences were provided by specialised gunners but when attacks began there was really very little the airmen could do. It was simply a case of taking shelter and waiting for the raid to finish:

> The Huns were out again tonight. We went into a ditch and got very muddy.[76]

In fictional tales of the aerial war – the Biggles stories in particular – pilots took great exception to attacks on their aerodromes and invariably set off on retaliation raids the minute the attack was over. Reality was very different. Bombing raids were viewed as an occupational hazard, something to be endured, knowing that next week or the week after the shoe would be on the other foot.

Death, of course, was always close, whether you were an airman or ground crew. Writing in clipped, insistent phrases that serve only to make the event more tragic and dramatic, Corporal G. R. Butt from 19 Squadron recounted in his diary one incident that happened at his own aerodrome:

> DH9, light fading at 5.20, hit the RE hangars at 100mph. It took the undercarriage off the machine. Turned over on the road, burst into flames – pyreenes. Ammunition exploded. Pilot burned to death. Observer rescued, two ribs broken.[77]

TRUTH IS STRANGER THAN FICTION

In a world where no airman could possibly know if he would still be alive at the end of the day, amazing risks were taken by pilots and observers alike. Some men seemed to bear charmed lives, surviving hundreds of hours in aerial combat and being shot down four, five or six times during their career. Others died within the first few hours of joining their Squadrons. W. E. Johns, creator of the Biggles stories, was clear that, to misquote Shakespeare, 'there are stranger things in Heaven and earth, Horatio'. To him:

> The speed at which a dog-fight took place and the amazing manner in which machines appeared from nowhere, and could disappear, apparently into thin air, was so bewildering as to baffle description. It is beyond my ability to

A crashed SE5 is examined by mechanics and pilots.

convey adequately the sensation of being one of ten or a dozen machines, zooming, whirling and diving among a maze of pencil-lines that marked the track of tracer bullets.[78]

In the early days of the war, when combat took place it was usually between single aircraft. With the development of fighter planes, more and more aircraft were drawn into huge air battles, melees that were quickly given the epithet 'dogfights'. By 1917 and 1918 dogfights between forty or fifty aeroplanes were fairly commonplace. They happened all the time. That did not stop them being a terrifying experience, for newcomers and experienced pilots alike:

Started off with formation at 12.15, absolutely looking for trouble - - - Having fooled about for some time we at last 'clicked.' They did not see us coming. Our leader, a survivor of many nifty scraps, took us up between the sun and them. Our leader gave the Hun sign and then we dived and went slick into the middle of them. My aunt, what a mix – Huns and Camels all over the place. Poor old Fritz died of fright. So did I, on the quiet. I just followed my leader all over the place and fired madly at any Hun I saw. Once I heard Hun guns behind me – simply charged around. Two of our fellows, Clarke and Lindsey, priceless fellows, got a Hun each.[79]

There are dozens of stories about pilots firing at point blank range, emptying their guns into enemy aircraft without causing the slightest damage. And sometimes the effect of machine gun fire or Archie was delayed:

Pilots who were shot down had a reasonable chance of survival as long as they were able to keep control of their damaged machines. If they went into a spin or the aircraft caught fire then they had no chance whatsoever. This shows a crashed German fighter in the ruins of the Houthulst Forest.

> Archie damn good. Lt Spence leading. We strafed a bridge; he also dived on a two seater - - - We started for our lines at about 500 feet. I kept close to him as we were getting hell from the ground. Suddenly he burst into flames and crashed about two miles west of Courthiezy. Poor devil. I'm damn sorry. He was a good chap. He crashed in Hun land – it was a rotten sight.[80]

No story is more remarkable than the well-known tale of Louis Strange and his lucky escape from death early in 1915. Flying an unwieldy Martinsyde single-seater with a machine gun mounted on the top wing, Strange found himself in one-to-one combat with a German Aviatik.

After firing a full drum of ammunition at the Aviatik, without effect, Strange had to reload his gun. He stood up in the cockpit and pulled hard at the empty ammunition drum. He lost his balance and before he knew what happening he found the Martinsyde flying upside down. His safety belt snapped and Strange was thrown out of the aeroplane, dangling in the air but holding on to the empty ammunition drum. It was all that kept him and the plane in contact.

With superhuman effort Louis Strange managed to swing his legs back into the cockpit and, with the Martinsyde now spinning towards the ground, regain control of the aircraft. Every instrument in the Martinsyde was broken or smashed but Louis Strange did not have a bruise or a cut anywhere on his body.

A Martinsyde F4 fighter, the type of machine flown by Louis Strange when he had his remarkable escape from death.

The German ace Boelcke once encountered a British RE8 flying sedately towards Germany. Both the pilot and the observer were dead in their cockpits but the plane kept flying on an even keel through the sky. Boelcke watched it go, driving on until, supposedly, it eventually ran out of fuel and crashed.

Manfred von Richthofen was probably already dead when he managed to land his Fokker Triplane behind British lines in April 1918. Whether the aeroplane was stable enough to land itself with a dead pilot at the controls or Richthofen managed in his last moments of consciousness to put the machine down will never be known. These days forensic examination would probably tell us but in 1918 such skills were light years away.

The death of James McCudden VC in a simple accident after four years of aerial warfare remains virtually unexplainable. On his way to assume command of a fighter Squadron in France – having flown across the Channel – he stopped to ask directions before taking off once more. McCudden's SE5 simply fell out of the air, killing the man hundreds of German pilots had tried to destroy and failed, dismally.

Sometimes it seemed as if fate was conspiring against the pilots. Captain W. E. Johns told the story of one ill-fated airman:

It was 'H', a tall South African SE pilot, who came in white faced and told me he had just shot down a Camel by mistake. It was the Camel pilot's fault. He playfully zoomed over the SE, apparently out of sheer light-heartedness. 'H' told me he started shooting when he saw the shadow; he turned and saw the red, white and blue circles, but it was too late - - - (He) fired a burst of not more than five rounds. He had fired hundreds of rounds at enemy aircraft without hitting one, but the Camel fell in flames. He asked me if he should report it and I, rightly or wrongly, said no, for nothing could bring the Camel back. 'H' went west soon afterwards.[81]

Small wonder, then, that most airmen of the Great War believed that truth certainly was stranger than fiction.

8

BLOODY APRIL

The month of April 1917 has gone down in history as the period with the worst casualty figures recorded by the RFC in the entire war.

In 1916 it had been estimated by the War Office that the average life expectancy for aircrew in France was two and a half months for fighter pilots, and four months for those flying two-seater reconnaissance machines. That meant a casualty rate of about 230 per cent. However, once the Germans introduced their DIII Albatross in the early months of 1917 things immediately began to change.

The new Albatross was a much improved fighter with a superbly robust engine and V struts on the wings that made it instantly recognisable to pilots of all sides. In the hands of men like von Richthofen, it cut a swathe right through the heart of the RFC and soon the casualty figure for British pilots had increased to 400 per cent. During 'Bloody April' that figure rose again, this time to 600 per cent, a life expectancy of under two months for all pilots on the Western Front.[82]

With such a casualty rate, training squadrons could not hope to cope with the demands for more men and many young pilots were sent out to France with just a bare handful of flying hours in their log books. Many of these

The favourite aeroplane of many flyers, the Sopwith Pup.

An RFC equipment officer issues guns and ammunition to pilots before a patrol.

A Sopwith Camel waiting for take-off – note the distinctive 'hump' in front of the cockpit that gave the aircraft its name.

replacement pilots had not even unpacked their kit when, on their first or second trip across the lines, they were shot down and killed. They were simply no match for hardened battle experts like the pilots of von Richthofen's Jasta.

Part of the trouble stemmed from Hugh Trenchard's policy of offensive patrols deep into enemy territory. Such a policy took no account of the fact that the German Albatross and Halberstadt fighters were markedly superior to the Sopwith Pups and Triplanes. Also the Battle of Arras began early in the month of April and the RFC was obliged to support the ground attack with reconnaissance and offensive patrols from its fighter Squadrons, invariably operating many miles over German-held territory.

By the time the Battle of Arras finished in May 1917 well over 200 RFC aircraft had been lost in action, their aircrew either killed or taken prisoner – German losses, in contrast, were under a hundred. The arrival of new British aircraft did manage to put a stop to the German onslaught but it had been a very close run thing for the RFC.

ACES HIGH

By the autumn of 1916, with the war on the ground having descended into a stalemate, the advent of the air ace was a godsend to newspapers and propaganda units alike – so much so that the period between the summer of 1916 and August 1917 has been called 'the year of the aces'. It was certainly a time when the concept of aerial aces really impinged itself on the minds of the public and men like von Richthofen and George Guynemer first became household names.

The early German ace Parschau, a man who learned to fly before the war and, in his Fokker Eindekker, claimed six victories before he was killed over Grevillers on 21 July 1916.

Captain Albert Ball VC, the first British pilot to grab the interest and imagination of the public. No strategist, Ball attacked his opponents head on, relying on them flinching first and turning away. With such tactics it was inevitable that, sooner or later, he would be killed.

As far as the papers and the public were concerned, the aces, at least, fought a 'good war' with victory and defeat clearly evident. They were the Hectors and Lysanders, the Achilles, the Ajax and the Hannibals, of modern warfare – they were the 'knights of the air'.

The trouble with building up heroes was having to cope with the grief and pain they caused when they were brought down. So while the newspapers were happy to brag about the victories of French 'ace of aces', Georges Guynemer, they were not so content to comment on his death when he was finally shot down. A whole generation of French children was brought up on the belief that Guynemer had simply flown so high he could never come down.

The thought that a nation's hero or champion could be bested by another was not to be contemplated. National pride was at stake and rather than admit a particular warrior was beaten by a better man or a superior machine, it was considered more appropriate to gloss over the death.

Albert Ball, one of the earliest British aces, it was said, flew into a cloud and never reappeared. Yet anyone who flew with him was clear that Ball's tactics of charging, bull-headed at the enemy without worry or concern about his own safety would, inevitably, end up with his death.

The Royal Flying Corps and, as it became after April 1918, the Royal Air Force could boast no fewer than 784 aces, men with more than five kills to their credit. Of this elite group fourteen were credited with more than forty victories. Germany had 363 pilots who could claim more than five victories, France 158.[83]

Both Germany and France grouped their ace pilots into elite Squadrons but, clearly, the British system of spreading the better pilots through the service and hoping that their skills and talents would rub off on others was a more effective way forward. The pilots of the RFC knew it and were, in the main, more than happy with the situation:

> Of course there were dangerous Huns about, circuses like Richthofen's, but they weren't met frequently on that Front, and the German habit of draining their best pilots away into circuses left the ordinary people very ordinary.[84]

BRITISH ACES

Albert Ball was the first great British ace. He was quiet and reserved, a shy man who was deeply religious and loved nothing better than talking about flower and vegetable growing or, in the evenings when others were drinking in the Mess, playing his violin. That was when he was off duty, on the ground. In the air Ball was like a madman, throwing his Nieuport (and, later, SE5) around and charging directly at the enemy, knowing that they would eventually panic and swerve. Then Ball would fasten onto their tails and shoot them down.

Albert Ball loved to fly alone, returning to his aerodrome with his plane full of rips and bullet holes. His official tally was forty-seven victories but was probably far greater; his lone exploits meant that, in many cases, his victories could not be confirmed.

The stories about Ball are legendary. The most famous concerns a challenge he made to two German pilots, dropping a note telling them he considered them to have acted in a cowardly way. He would meet them over their aerodrome next day, he said, when they could settle the matter like gentlemen. Of course, Ball flew into a trap. Five enemy machines were waiting for him but Albert Ball kept them at bay until he finally ran out of ammunition.

In desperation, Ball flung his Nieuport into a spin. The German fliers, thinking he had been hit, followed him down at a more leisurely pace. When Ball straightened out and landed in a field, the Germans came down as well, hoping to take prisoner this, the greatest of British aces. Ball was now slumped over in his cockpit but as the Germans ran up to his machine he suddenly sat up, opened the throttle and zoomed back into the sky. He had not even received a scratch.[85]

James McCudden, Jimmy as he was known throughout the service, had joined the RFC before the war, serving as a mechanic and travelling out to France with the first aeroplanes of No. 3 Squadron. He progressed to flight training after serving as an observer, eventually winning the Victoria Cross for his bravery, rising to the rank of Major and to the command of No. 60 Squadron. He could not quite escape the stigma of being 'born in barracks',

In contrast to Ball, James McCudden was a tactician and strategist par excellence. He was a superb shot and knew all there was to know about his – and the enemy – machines. In the end he was killed in a simple accident, not enemy action.

Edward 'Mick' Mannock was, possibly, the greatest air fighter of the war, yet such was the reluctance of the RFC to recognise or publicise its aces, he was unknown to the British public until after the war. Like von Richthofen he was shot down and killed by ground fire.

however, and was actually rejected as commanding officer by one Squadron, more snobbish than the rest, because of his lowly origins.

As an air fighter he had no equal, constantly fiddling with his engine and guns in order to achieve the maximum effect. He had no hatred of the Germans but saw what he was doing as a job, something that had to be done – at least until one evening patrol when he shot down an Albatross in flames:

> At once a little trickle of flame came out of his fuselage, which became larger and larger until the whole fuselage and tail plane was enveloped in flames - - - That was my first Hun in flames. As soon as I saw it I thought 'Poor devil,' and really felt sick. It was at that time revolting to see any machine go down in flames, especially when it was done by my own hands.[86]

Edward 'Mick' Mannock was possibly the greatest British ace of the whole war. Like Jimmy McCudden, he was of Irish origin and the son of a serving soldier – who deserted the family as soon as he was able, leaving the young Edward to be brought up by his mother and siblings.

After a difficult childhood, Mannock became an engineer with a telephone company, taking a job in Turkey and, once Turkey joined the war on the side of Germany, was interned in a POW camp. He spent several months as a prisoner, only being released because his physical condition – he had a congenital defect in his left eye – almost guaranteed that he would never take up arms against the Central Powers. How wrong the Turks were.

Repatriated and recovered, Mick Mannock joined the Army Medical Corps, transferred to the Royal Engineers and finally found a niche for himself as a pilot in the RFC. Quite how he managed to pass the rigorous physical examination – the eye test in particular – remains something of a mystery but pass he did:

> When the Adjutant sent for me today and informed me of my transfer to the RFC I could have kissed him, although he has the most repulsive 'mug' of any man that I have ever met. Yes! I could have kissed it; such was my unbounded delight. Now for the Bosche! I am going to strive to become a scout pilot like Ball. Watch me. I wonder what fate has in store?[87]

Amazingly, early opinions about Mannock were that he was a little 'over careful' with his personal safety – not a coward but not the stuff of heroes either. It was two months before he shot down his first German aeroplane but in that time he had perfected his shooting and skill as a pilot. Within three weeks he had shot down five more and now there was no longer any thought or talk of cowardice.

Mannock was a fervent patriot who developed a violent and vitriolic hatred for the enemy. He loved nothing better than to see German aircraft falling to earth wrapped in flames – although it was a death he feared and carried a pistol in his pocket in order to shoot himself should his plane ever catch fire. There is a famous story about him refusing to drink a toast proposed by fellow ace Rhys Davids to Manfred von Richthofen: 'I won't drink a toast to that son of a bitch,' he declared. And he meant it.

Like von Richthofen, Mannock grew to be a great individual fighter pilot and an even greater leader. Although he was officially credited with seventy-three victories (sixteen more than his great friend and mentor James McCudden and seven less than von Richthofen) he undoubtedly scored many more. It became standard procedure for him to damage an enemy machine, and then stand aside to allow a new pilot to gain the credit for his first kill – exactly what he was doing when he was finally shot down, in flames, by ground fire in June 1918.

There were many more aces of note in the RFC. Men like the Canadians Billy Bishop and Billy Barker, the Australian R. S. Dallas, Welshmen Rhys Davids and Ira 'Taffy' Jones, and Raymond Collishaw of the RNAS achieved enormous victory tallies that ensured for them places of honour in the histories of their Squadrons.

Arthur Rhys-Davids, the man who shot down Werner Voss, is shown here in a painting by official war artist Sir William Orpen.

FRENCH ACES

René Fonck was the leading French ace, shooting down an official total of seventy-five enemy machines. However, his own estimation was much higher; Fonck claimed to have despatched no fewer than 127 German machines. If this figure is true it would make him the highest scoring ace on either side.

Born in the Vosges Region of France, Fonck trained as a pilot and was posted, first, to a Squadron flying old fashioned and out-dated Caudron G1Vs. Despite this he managed to shoot down two German aircraft and in April 1917 he was duly posted to Group de Combat No. 12, flying SPAD fighters. Thereafter his score mounted rapidly.

Fonck was an aloof, taciturn man who was not particularly well-liked by his fellow pilots. He was, however, a fine marksman, a superb deflection shot and someone who preferred to fly and fight alone. A hunter of the Richthofen class, it was not unusual for him to return to base having fired only a dozen or so rounds but with a number of confirmed victories to his credit.[88]

Fonck overtook Guynemer as the leading French ace on 1 August 1918 and on 26 September he destroyed six enemy machines in one patrol – and then ran out of ammunition. He was a cool tactical fighter pilot, engaging in combat

René Fonck, the leading French ace, was credited with seventy-five victories. He believed his tally was considerably higher. He survived the war, dying in 1953.

only when conditions and situations suited him. Fonck survived the war, dying in 1953 as a venerable and much respected veteran.

If Fonck was self contained and aloof, Charles Nungesser was the opposite. He was a happy and cheerful man who would fight all day and then slip off to Paris for an evening in the bars of Montmarte. Renowned as a boxer in the days before the outbreak of war, by the end of 1914 he had already won several medals for gallantry.

Transferring to the flying service, Nungesser began by crashing his Morane, breaking both his legs and suffering internal injuries. Although he could barely walk, needing two sticks to help him move about, Nungesser was soon flying again and beginning to score regular victories.

Nungesser was a natural pilot but, despite his ability, he still managed to regularly crash his SPAD. In between crashes he was gradually extending his tally, eventually accounting for forty-five German planes.

Nungesser's natural vivacity and desire to live life to the full made him a perfect companion for the young American pilots who, by the simple procedure of joining the French Foreign Legion, became eligible to fight for France and made up the Escadrille Lafayette (Escadrille Americaine as it was first called). These 'soldiers of fortune' who wanted to help in the war against German aggression accounted for 199 victories before, with America's entry into the war, they were incorporated into the United States Air Force.[89]

The French 'ace of aces', although his victory tally was twenty-one short of René Fonck, was the immortal Georges Guynemer. A sickly child who grew into a sickly adult, Guynemer was rejected on three occasions for military service and was eventually obliged to call on family influence (the Guynemers had been influential in government and military circles since the time of Napoleon) in order to obtain his commission.

Guynemer was a perfectionist. He studied his aircraft until he knew every nut and bolt of the machine. He made himself into a fine shot but, like Albert Ball, had little time for strategy and tactics. He attacked the enemy head on, charging at them as if he was going to chop them into pieces with his propeller.

The French public fell in love with the frail, almost gentle Guynemer – gentle on the ground, that is. Newspapers wrote articles about him and, for a time, it seemed as if his photograph was constantly in front of every French man and woman.

When he went to Paris, Guynemer was mobbed by the public, women in particular. Yet, by September 1917, he was living on borrowed time. His nerves were as taut as a bowstring and, even though shellshock and post-traumatic syndrome were unknown quantities at that time, it was clear to everyone that Georges Guynemer needed a rest. He was destined never to get it.

Guynemer knew, of course, what the end result would be. When asked by one adoring woman what other decoration he could win his reply was simple – 'The wooden cross'.[90]

The French 'ace of aces' was
Georges Guynemer, a man
who found incredible fame and
popularity with the French public.

Guynemer was a quiet, gentle man,
delicate and almost effeminate in
his mannerisms – on the ground.
In the air he flew and fought
like a madman, charging at the
enemy until they turned away in
desperation. Like Albert Ball, his
death was almost inevitable.

DANS LE NORD — Le Capitaine aviateur Guynemer,
venant de recevoir l'ordre belge de Léopold Militaire,
des mains du roi Albert Ier.

There were other French pilots, men like Georges Madon and René Dorme, but none of them ever had the appeal of Georges Guynemer. To the French public he really was the ace of aces.

GERMAN ACES

Manfred von Richthofen was the highest scoring fighter pilot of the war, shooting down eighty Allied aircraft, most of them British and forty-six of them being lumbering two-seater reconnaissance planes. He has been criticised for this but Richthofen was fighting a war – and he was fighting to win. Spotter aircraft had to be eliminated and Richthofen, a natural hunter, was just the man to do it.

Born in Breslau, Manfred and his brother Lothar spent their holidays on the family country estate and, thanks to hours spent hunting in the woods, became excellent shots. Richthofen went to war as an officer with an Uhlan cavalry regiment and did, in fact, lead a cavalry charge against the French in the early war of movement. Once the conflict had settled into the static grind of trench warfare, he became bored and began looking for other ways to enjoy himself. The flying service offered the prospect of excitement and good hunting that he was looking for.

To some extent von Richthofen was lucky. His graduation from cavalry officer to observer to pilot came at a time when Germany was beginning to regain control of the skies over France, thanks in no small degree to new aircraft like the Albatross D11. And soon Richthofen's victory tally began to mount. After the death of Boelcke, Jagstaffel No. 2 was renamed the Boelcke Jagstaffel in his honour, led now by Hans Kirmaier, and Richthofen became one of its star pilots. It was a time of great adventure for the young pilots and the counting of victories was akin to gaining trophies on the hunting field:

> At this time I was trying to compete with Jagstaffel Boelcke. In the evenings we compared our mutual bags. There were some devilish fellows there, and they were never to be outdone - - - The chances for victory all depend on which opponent one faces – the sneaky Frenchman or those plucky fellows, the Englishmen. I prefer the Englishmen. The Frenchman flinches, the Englishman seldom does.[91]

Von Richthofen soon decided to paint his Albatross bright red. It was something he later did with his favourite aircraft, the Fokker Triplane, but even he did not really know why he should make his aeroplanes quite so distinctive. Yet he was totally aware of the effect it had, both on his own comrades and on the enemy:

Manfred von Richtofen, the highest scoring ace of the war, a man with eighty kills to his name. He is shown here with General von Hoeppner, commander of the German flying services.

Der kommandierende General der Luftstreitkräfte Exz. von Hoeppner beglückwünscht Rittmeister Frhr. von Richthofen.

One day, for no particular reason, I got the idea to paint my crate glaring red. After that, absolutely everyone knew my red bird - - - One of the Englishmen we had shot down was taken prisoner and we went over to talk to him. He, too, inquired about the red machine. It was not unknown to the troops in the trenches who called it 'Le diable rouge'. The rumour had spread in his Squadron that a girl piloted the red machine, somewhat like Joan of Arc. He was very surprised when I assured him that the alleged 'girl' stood before him.[92]

In June 1917 Richthofen was given command of Jagdgeschwader No. 1, a decision that was greeted with enthusiasm from the German pilots. Four Jastas, Nos 4, 6, 10 and 11, comprised this battle group. Richthofen was respected and admired but he was a cold, distant person who found difficulty in relating to his comrades. He was not universally popular like the handsome Bruno Loerzer or even his own younger brother Lothar. When Loerzer, Udet, Goering and the rest gathered to sing around the piano in the evenings, Manfred von Richthofen invariably sat alone, his mind already planning the following day's hunt.

Ernst Udet was second only to von Richthofen, destroying sixty-two enemy planes and surviving the war. Born in 1896, Udet had always been fascinated by aeroplanes and, in the days before 1914, even built himself a glider – which he promptly crashed. Too short to be accepted by the military, he served as a volunteer motorbike messenger, and then took private flying lessons – after which he was immediately accepted into the German Air Service.

Flying a two-seater Aviatik, Udet won himself the Iron Cross, 2nd Class, when he and his observer nursed their damaged plane back home, the observer having to crawl out onto the wing in order to balance the damaged aircraft. Udet transferred to a fighter Squadron and had already achieved twenty victories when he was spotted by von Richthofen and asked to join Jagdgeschwader No 1. Soon he had risen to command Jasta 11, Richthofen's old unit, within the Jagdgeschwader.

There were personality clashes with Herman Goering, who eventually rose to take Richthofen's command and Udet did actually query some of the victory claims Goering made in these latter years of the war. It was a clash that would come back to haunt Udet.

Ernst Udet became one of the first pilots to save his life through the use of a parachute. On 29 June 1918, after a clash with a French fighter, he was forced to 'bale out'. The parachute did not open until he was 250 feet from the ground and Udet sprained his ankle in the fall. But the parachute certainly saved his life.

Perhaps the most famous story about Udet concerns the French ace Guynemer. They encountered each other one day and immediately became involved in a one-to-one combat. Just as Udet got the Frenchman in his sights his guns jammed and nothing he could do would clear them. Realising what had happened, Guynemer flew alongside his opponent for a while, then waved and flew away. A few weeks later Guynemer was killed in combat.

Werner Voss was probably the most respected of all the German flyers. He was, pilots of the RFC believed, quite as skilful as Richthofen, his Triplane being easily identified by the skull and crossbones he painted on the nose of the silver machine.

A brave and resourceful man, he once landed in No Man's Land in order to prize off a piece of the machine he had just shot down. Shelled and machine gunned, Voss got his proof of the kill and just managed to get back into the air. He was credited with forty-eight victories but there is no doubt that, had he not fought his last – and greatest – battle against overwhelming odds, he would have added many more to his tally.

Germany had many more aces of note, pilots like Bruno Loerzer – a Jasta leader to rival Richthofen himself. Then there were Berthold and Lowenhardt and even the Red Baron's brother Lothar who many considered a finer pilot – and certainly one who was a lot more personable.

Ernst Udet was second only to von Richthofen, accounting for sixty-two enemy aircraft. Udet used a parachute to escape from his burning aircraft in 1918 and survived the war, rising to a high position in the German Air Ministry before committing suicide in 1941.

Reckless, dashing and brave, Werner Voss was admired by all Allied pilots. He is shown here with his commander, Manfred von Richthofen, standing in front of an Albatross fighter – Voss himself always preferred the Fokker Triplane.

OTHER ACES

Of course there were dozens of other pilots who, because of their personalities and skill, soon made names for themselves. Britain had one in Arthur Rhys Davids, a man who James McCudden considered the finest natural pilot he had ever seen. Germany had men like Hans Wolff and the disabled Karjus who, amazingly, had only one arm but shot better than most men with two. And then, of course, there were the pilots of countries like Belgium and the USA.

Willie Coppens was the top Belgian ace, a man who specialised in shooting down observation balloons, an occupation most sane men stayed well clear of. His victory tally was thirty-seven and, of these, no fewer than twenty-eight were balloons.

Coppens began his flying career at the end of 1915 but as he spent some of this time piloting two-seaters, most of his victories came during a seven month period in 1918, when he was finally given a Nieuport and then a French Hanriot to fly. He was severely wounded by incendiary bullets on 14 October that year and eventually had to have his leg amputated. It ended his flying career but despite this he lived until 1986.

Belgian's other ace of note was Edmond Thieffry. An Attorney before the war he quickly joined up when Belgium was invaded, was captured and managed to escape by riding a German motorbike over the border into neutral Holland. After being interned for a while he was released and joined the Belgian Flying Corps where he held the distinction of crashing more aircraft than any other Belgian trainee pilot. On one occasion a reflex reaction in his hands opened fire on the men who had come to pull him out of the wreck. They promptly dived for cover.

It was feared that Thieffry would certainly kill any observer who was assigned to fly with him. As a consequence he was posted to a single-seater fighter Squadron where he quickly achieved a total of ten victories. He himself was shot down in flames in February 1918 but survived the ordeal and spent the rest of the war in a POW camp.

Most of the American aces were men who, desperate to help the Allies in what they saw as a war against German aggression, had joined the French Foreign Legion and therefore managed to get themselves sent to the Lafayette Escadrille. Joining the Foreign Legion was essential as the US government had already announced that any man swearing an oath of loyalty to any country other than the USA would lose his American citizenship. The Legion demanded no oath of loyalty or allegiance, merely a statement that all of its members would promise to obey the orders of superior officers.[93]

Dr Edmund Gros, an American living and working in Paris, and Norman Prince from Massachusetts were the prime movers in putting together a group of pilots – or would-be pilots – who were quickly sent off to Pau for training. On 17 April 1916, the Escadrille Americaine (later Lafayette) came into existence. The original Squadron consisted of men like Victor Chapman,

Shooting down observation balloons became something of a speciality for Belgian ace Willie Coppens – he destroyed twenty-eight of them in a brief career of just seven months.

ADJUTANT E. THIEFFRY. THE WONDERFUL BELGI...

Belgium's other ace of note, Edmond Thieffry, was such a reckless pilot that it was inevitable he would be posted to a fighter squadron – otherwise he would surely have killed every observer who ever flew with him.

Kiffin Rockwell, Elliot Cowdin and Bert Hall. They were quickly augmented by a second wave and included here was America's first air ace, Raoul Lufbery.

Lufbery had already been serving in a French unit and he soon became the most skilled pilot in the Escadrille. He, along with Bert Hall and Bill Thaw, were instrumental in finding the Squadron's mascot, a lion cub called Whiskey. They paid 250 francs for the creature in Paris and over time the lion became almost as famous as the members of Escadrille Lafayette itself.[94]

When America entered the war Dr Gros was commissioned as a Lieutenant Colonel in the United States Air Force and set about obtaining transfers for men of the Escadrille Lafayette to the air force of the USA. Together with Colonel Billy Mitchell, Chief of Air Service, 1st Army Corps – and later the man in charge of all American Air Services – he set about creating a flying corps that could make a real difference to the aerial war.

By now Raoul Lufbery had seventeen victories to his name. After a period spent as an instructor to the new American flyers, Lufbery was finally posted to the 94th Squadron, the famous hat-in-the-ring Squadron, as Commanding Officer. He taught the new American pilots all he knew and while his young, impressionable charges thought him indestructible, he knew that his time was limited. When asked once what he would do after the war, Lufbery responded with the phrase, 'There won't be any after the war for a fighter pilot.'

He had always advised pilots to stay with a burning plane, to try side slipping and diving in an attempt to put out the flames. And then, on 19 May 1918, he forgot

The Lafayette Escadrille was made up of Americans who had joined the French Foreign Legion in order to fight in the war. This artist's impression shows them attacking a German supply base – over 100 Allied aircraft took part in the raid.

Raoul Lufbery, the first American ace, served with the Lafayette Escadrille before transferring to the US Air Corps once America entered the war. He had seventeen confirmed victories before his death in May 1918.

to follow his own advice. As he shot down a German two-seater, the men of his Squadron were horrified to see flames licking from the side of Lufbery's Nieuport. He lost height but the flames just grew and, finally, Luf – as his men called him – leapt out. He was aiming for a stream but missed and fell to his death.[95]

Eddie Rickenbacker was one of Lufbery's bright young stars. Before the war he was successful racing driver, possibly the most famous driver in America, and he brought his precise skill and fine eye to his new profession. Giving up his lucrative racing job, he was initially employed as a driver for Major Townsend Dodd, aviation advisor to General 'Black Jack' Pershing, commander of the US forces. That was until Billy Mitchell spotted him one day and had him transferred to flying duties. The rest, as they say, is history.

Rickenbacker's skill as a racing driver was replicated in his performance as a pilot. He knew that just one mistake could spell the end of everything and he was determined never to make that mistake. After one early escape from death he had his mechanics paint Maltese Crosses over three bullet holes beneath his cockpit – a reminder, if ever one was needed, of how close he had come to death. Keep alert at all times, was his constant mantra to himself. Equally as important, he passed on this advice to the men of his flight and, when promoted to be CO of the 94th Squadron, to all of his pilots.

A superb mechanic, Rickenbacker was also a pilot and an ace of some skill. He was determined not to be relegated to a desk job when he took command of the 94th and the very day the posting became official he was up before breakfast and shot down two enemy machines in less than an hour.

He is credited with twenty-six victories. In reality there were many more but, like Mick Mannock, he would regularly credit new pilots with kills that were

Eddie Rickenbacker, the top American ace, is shown here in front of his SPAD fighter – the 'hat in the ring' emblem of the US 94th squadron clearly visible on the side of the aircraft. A racing driver before the war, Rickenbacker went on to lead an adventurous and dramatic life in the years after the conflict ended.

really his. Perhaps the most amazing thing of all is the fact that Rickenbacker chalked up his kills in a brief seven month period, two months of which were spent in hospital and then recovering from a mastoid operation.

Frank Luke was, in the eyes of many Allied pilots, a typical American – loud, opinionated, undisciplined and with incredible belief in his own ability. Even his fellow pilots at No. 24 Squadron considered him a big mouth and a boaster. What many seemed to forget or overlook was that he was also damned good at what he did.

Within a brief window of seventeen days, Luke destroyed fifteen observation balloons and three enemy aircraft. In a personal crusade that, eventually, consumed him, Frank Luke was a one-man air force that infuriated his superiors as much as enthralled them. Two of his flying partners had been shot down and Luke took their deaths personally. And, of course, his own last fight has gone down in folklore.

On 19 September 1918 he destroyed three balloons and two German aircraft near the village of Murvaux and then strafed a group of soldiers on the ground. His SPAD was damaged and Luke himself was now seriously wounded. In an affidavit drawn up by the Mayor of Murvaux, it is clear that Frank Luke died the way he had lived – with energy, courage, self belief and enthusiasm:

> He landed and got out of his machine, undoubtedly to quench his thirst at the stream. He had gone fifty yards when, seeing the Germans come towards him, he still had the strength to draw his revolver to defend himself. A moment after, he fell dead following a serious wound he received in the chest.[96]

9

THOSE WHO ARE ABOUT TO DIE

While the casualties sustained by the airmen of the Great War were minimal when compared to those of the armies fighting on the ground, it has to be remembered that there were far fewer flyers than soldiers. Everything was relative and, for many, serving in one of the flying corps meant little more than a death sentence:

> We used to meet some of the airmen from the local 'drome at the estaminet in the village. And they were great blokes, young men just like us. But the difference was, they all knew they were going to die, sooner or later. Us? We knew there was a risk but we were artillery and unless an unlucky shell landed too close we had a better than even chance of surviving. Not those guys. They knew they weren't going to make it. I remember one of them, a bloke from Newcastle, laughing and giving us the old gladiator line – "Those who are about to die salute you."[97]

GENERAL JOFFRE INSPECTING A GERMAN ALBATROSS JUST 'DOWNED'

General Joffre takes a close look at an Albatross two-seater.

An Albatross fighter is brought down by Archie fire, engine full on, tail plane and wing smashed. The end result is inevitable.

Such a fatalistic attitude was rife in all of the air services. If your number was up, your number was up – there was no point worrying. That's not to say they didn't have concerns and fears but most of the young pilots and navigators kept those fears hidden – as much as they were able. Only in their letters and diaries were they really able to express themselves. And it was often the death of a friend or comrade that provoked the deep response:

> Patrol at 10.30 and 12.15. When I landed there was some ghastly news. Poor Fish, who used to come into Calais with us, was seen to be hit in the air by one of our fellows. He fell at Poperinghe. I've never felt so sick in my life. Poor old Fish, MC and Bar. And such a good chap. It's taken all the guts out of me for flying. I'm so miserable and jumpy these days. Another job tonight.[98]

In public, in the Mess, such sentiments could never be shown. An unwritten law quickly established itself – you did not mourn lost comrades, you drank their health and, quite often, drank yourself into oblivion as well.

Concert parties and trips to the local estaminet were fine enough – members of the RFC and the German Air Service had more opportunity than most serving soldiers to enjoy their delights – but alcohol was the means most airmen chose to push away their fears. The stories of Public School-style binges in the Mess are legendary, creating a tradition that lasted up to and beyond the Battle of Britain

A fighter pilot lies dead in the wreckage of his smashed machine, one of the many victims of a brutal and bloody war.

in 1940. Destruction of plates and furniture was common, was accepted as the norm for most RFC Squadrons. It was a way of 'letting off steam'.

Shell shock – or neurasthenia as it was known – was a relatively new phenomenon. There are recorded cases of pilots suffering and being treated at places like Craiglockhart, where the poet Siegfried Sassoon was incarcerated for a while, but in reality, such was the individual nature of the airman's war, pilots suffering from nervous exhaustion were usually shot down and killed before they could be helped.

Even aces were not immune. Mick Mannock found it more and more difficult to disguise his badly worn nerves and everyone knew that Guynemer was close to the edge – and that was long before either of them was killed.

Part of the trouble was that, as an airman, you were never really out of the war, unless you were at home on leave. Even practice could be a dangerous business:

A fellow called Proudfoot was killed while practicing. He was diving at the ground target, engine full on, angle of dive about 45° when his machine was seen to suddenly dive vertically. Then it proceeded to go under the vertical. The machine seemed to stop and then the wings folded up - - - I saw Proudfoot flung out of the machine and fall, closely followed by the machine. Drysdale, Stock and myself rushed over to the place where it had crashed. The machine was in bits and poor Proudfoot was about ten feet away. He had hit a tree and bounced off. He was in pieces when we picked him up. Oh Lord, it makes you tired of war to see such awful things as that – here one minute, gone the next.[99]

King George V speaking to Lt Leonard Henry Rochford, RNAS – known throughout the service as 'Tich' – during a tour of inspection. Rochford had taught himself to fly when he was still too young to enlist but by 1918 was Flight Commander in No. 203 Squadron and had twenty-nine victories to his credit.

So was it luck or judgement that kept a pilot alive? The answer is probably a little bit of both. Certainly it was skill and ability that kept Jimmy McCudden safe through hundreds of dogfights and offensive patrols. Yet when he was killed, trying to turn back to the airfield when his engine failed, was that bad judgement or did his luck simply run out?

Arguably, poor judgement killed both Micky Mannock and Manfred von Richthofen. Both men had long stressed that pilots should never follow a damaged plane or a supposed kill to the floor – and yet that was precisely what both of them did, only to be hit by machine gun fire from the ground. Bad judgement? Or perhaps they had both pushed the limits, tested their luck, for a little too long.

Nobody, either then or now, has been able to legislate or explain why one man might be shot down four or five times and live and yet another might be killed on his first flight over the lines. There was no reason, no rationale:

It was difficult to assign reasons for survival - - - youth and immaturity of practical judgement were no doubt adverse factors; and then differences of eyesight and habitual alertness told; and lastly acquired tactical skill and innate cunning. But when all these things were allowed for, it was difficult amid the flying bullets to believe in anything but luck. Everyone got shot up occasionally, and nothing but luck could account for the inches this way or that which made a bullet harmless or fatal.[100]

OTHER THEATRES

Although the skies above the Western Front were clearly the crucible in which pilots were formed or destroyed, according to their luck and judgement, aircraft were also well used in many of the other theatres of war.

As early as the final months of 1914, German reconnaissance aircraft were proving their worth on the Russian or Eastern Front when they reported on troop movements during the Battle of Tannenberg. General Paul von Hindenburg was clear that without reconnaissance from the air the German victory would never have been achieved.

Gerhard Fieseler was one of the most successful fighter pilots in Macedonia with nineteen confirmed victories. Canadian ace William Barker scored twenty-seven of his fifty-three victories while serving with the RFC in Italy while the French air service provided a number of aircraft for the otherwise dormant campaign in Salonika.

When Baghdad was lost to Axis forces in March 1917, it was intended to send five air squadrons to support the German attempt to retake the city. In the event, due to the deteriorating German position in Palestine, these aircraft were diverted to the Holy Land. By March 1918 the Germans had over 300 aircraft operating in Macedonia and the Middle East. Naturally, British and French aircraft had to be diverted from the Western Front in order to counter their presence.

German aircraft had already been active in Palestine. On 3 November 1916 a Rumpler C1, piloted by Leutnant Schultheiss, had flown from Birseba to

The Italian Air Service fought mainly against the airmen of Austria-Hungary. They were supported by numerous units from the RFC.

First World War in the Air

French aircraft sit on their airfield in Salonika. The campaign was moribund from the beginning and the aircraft had little or no role to play.

The engine from a damaged aircraft being brought back to base from the crash site in Egypt's desert – real Camels this time!

drop bombs on the railway station in Cairo. A photograph of the aircraft high over the Pyramids – even though the image of the plane was superimposed onto the photograph at a later date – was well used for propaganda purposes by the Germans.

The combined Turkish–German assault on the Suez Canal at the end of 1916 was supported by German aircraft but the attack came to nothing. With pressure mounting in France, new machines and new German pilots were increasingly sent to the Western Front. Naturally enough, British and French forces followed suit.

THE AIR WAR IN LITERATURE

Considering the amount of poetry that came out of the Great War, it is perhaps surprising that very little quality verse was written and published by airmen. The reasons for this are hard to identify but perhaps it had something to do with the fact that the war, as fought by the airmen, was constant. Unlike their soldier counterparts, there were no extended periods out of the lines, on rest, and that was when most of the soldier's poetry was written.

Perhaps the most famous 'flying' poem of the war was written by a non-combatant, a man who had little sympathy either with the war poets or with Britain's war aims – W. B. Yeats' 'An Irish Airman Foresees his Death'. It is a wonderful reconstruction but it is hardly an original RFC poem and Yeats cannot avoid his political convictions creeping in:

I know that I shall meet my fate
Somewhere among the clouds above;
Those that I fight I do not hate,
Those that I guard I do not love.[101]

Jeffrey Day was an RNAS pilot of some renown, winning the DFC and having a number of victories to his credit. He was killed in combat on 27 February 1918 and his sole poetry book, *Poems and Rhymes*, was not published until 1919. His most celebrated poem was 'On the Wings of the Morning', published first in *The Cornhill*. It might not be in the class of Wilfred Owen or Sassoon but, as a poet, Day certainly had some skill. Sadly he did not live to exploit it:

My turning wing inclines towards the ground;
The ground itself glides up with graceful swing
and at the plane's far tip twirls slowly round,
then drops from sight again beneath the wing
to slip away serenely as before,
a cubist-patterned carpet on the floor.[102]

EVENING POST
SPECIAL EDITION

IRMAN'S
GREAT
FEAT

WHAT YER LAUGHING AT?

One of the few humorous postcards about the RFC. There were dozens of witty cards about the Army and the conditions soldiers had to endure but, for some reason, the war in the air was not considered a funny topic.

Men like Gordon Alchin (who wrote under the pen name Observer) and Paul Brasher of the RNAS wrote poetry about their wartime experiences that have stood the test of time. It is often unpretentious stuff but heartfelt nonetheless:

> Sometimes I fly at dawn above the sea,
> Where, underneath, the restless waters flow –
> Silver, and cold, and slow.[103]

However, it is very difficult to take at all seriously some of the verse produced by airmen. Lines such as the following are nothing more than doggerel:

> Here in the eye of the sun
> I sit and wait for the Hun;
> Twenty thousand feet on high
> Out on the roof of the world am I.[104]

There was at least one other poetry book written by an airman, Lieutenant Louis Solomon, who was killed in early 1918. Entitled *Wooden Crosses and Other Poems*, the book was published in 1918 but seems to have disappeared from view. Certainly no poems by Solomon appear in any of the war anthologies and a phrase used in an obituary in *The Jewish Chronicle* might say something about the quality of the verse:

> It seems unlikely that a major poet could have been overlooked for so long; and the phrase "a keen sense of humour and a knack of versification which must have given a great deal of pleasure to his friends" may well indicate that Lt Solomon's was a very minor talent.[105]

Humour was much in evidence in the RFC Messes, particularly in the songs that the airmen sang. You might expect to find humorous verse in the pages of *The Wipers (or BEF) Times* but, sadly, the only poems of worth that have anything to do with aerial combat seem to be more to about the effect of the war on the Home Front than anything else:

> Hear now the howl of rage which rends
> The skies from Nieuport to Lorraine,
> Which wanders down the line and ends
> When breath has flown, and all are sane;
> Blanched faces, furtive looks and eyes
> Which show the horror felt by all,
> And fury at the sacrilege
> Holds everyone of us in thrall.
>
> And in each heart the certainty
> That soon the deed reward shall find,
> Just, swift and sure the payment be,
> And we to pity all are blind:
> He, with this infamy has topped
> A list of crimes which e'er must irk us,
> Who with a craven hand has dropped
> A bomb in Piccadilly Circus.[106]

Prose, however, is a very different matter. There are dozens of accounts written by pilots who managed to survive the war, even some by men such as McCudden and Richthofen who did not. Some of these, such as *The Wind in the Wires* by Duncan Grinnell-Milne and *Sagittarius Rising* by Cecil Lewis, have deservedly become classics in their own right. They are, however, memoirs, factual accounts of what each pilot remembers and thinks worth recording. For pieces of imaginative fiction we have to look a little deeper.

Winged Victory by Victor Yeates is probably the finest piece of creative prose ever written about aerial combat and its effects – and that includes both the First and Second World Wars. It is the story of one man and his struggle to survive, physically and emotionally, while serving in a Camel Squadron in the final year

French and British pilots line up for an inspection. The aircraft in the background are RE8 two-seater reconnaissance machines. Affectionately nick named 'Harry Tate', after the music hall star, its pilots considered the plane too slow to be an effective weapon of war but it remained in service, carrying out many artillery spotting missions, until the end of the conflict.

of the war. It is based on Yeates' own flying experiences and is made all the more poignant by the fact that he was dying of TB even as he wrote his amazing novel.

The pressures, tensions, fears and demands of life in a fighter squadron are brilliantly caught and outlined. The need not to show fear, to keep up appearances in front of colleagues, provides only extra strain. Tom Cundall, the hero of the book, is an ordinary enough man with all the concerns and terrors you would expect from someone living in constant touch with death. For a brief moment he thinks he has found a way out of the situation:

> The way out was so easy. It was only necessary to pick a quiet spot in Hunland, away from where you'd been bombing, and land there, and your war was over. The immediate future might not be very comfortable, but that was nothing. Who was to know? Your engine had cut out; you had been shot down; anything. The Germans weren't likely to be very interested; and if you had time to set your machine on fire after you had removed the spare razor and tooth brush which you always carried with you in case of accidents.[107]

At the end of the day, of course, Cundall is too decent a human being, too conscious of his duty and of his commitment to friends, to take that course of action. As Yeates says, 'But he hadn't a spare razor.'

No account of literature about First World War flying, however brief, would ever be complete without mention of the famous Biggles books. W. E. Johns, the

The dust jacket of *Biggles, Pioneer Air Fighter*, one of many popular flying stories by Capt W. E. Johns. Often derided because of the 'gung ho' attitudes of the characters, most of the young men who flew in the Battle of Britain were raised on the stories of the fictional Biggles and his friends.

writer, has often endured odium and, perhaps, unfair criticism for his creation and his many adventures. But it has to be remembered that, as we tend to read them these days, the stories were aimed at children and adolescents. This was certainly not the case when they were first published.

The original tales first saw the light of day in the magazine *Popular Flying*, with a clear adult readership. Many of the men who bought the magazine would have served in the RFC or RAF and for that reason alone they had to be accurate and realistic. It was not long, however, before publishers, with an eye to what had become a growth market, decided these stories were ideal for a younger audience. And so they were duly altered and amended when, of course, things like swearing and kissing your girlfriend had to be ruthlessly cut out:

> When he [Biggles] sees a Camel pilot heading for disaster he cries 'Great Scott! What's he doing?' Thirsty airmen develop an astonishing taste for lemonade – the crowning absurdity occurring when Biggles and his friend Wilks vie with each other to obtain some bottles of lemonade from a French hotelier, that had been specially imported for an Englishman before the war; the lemonade in the original story was pre-war whiskey.[108]

The Great War Biggles stories are acknowledged to be the best of Johns' vast output. And despite the publisher's (and Johns') tinkering with the text in order to fit in with the demands of his audience, they do contain some excellent descriptive passages that catch the time and moment quite beautifully:

> They took off together and circled over the aerodrome, climbing steadily for height - - - It was not an ideal day for observation. Great masses of detached cumulus cloud were sailing majestically eastward and through these Biggles threaded his way, the other Camel in close attendance. Sometimes through the cloud they could see the ground, and from time to time Biggles pointed out salient landmarks - - - Gradually the recognisable features became fewer until they were lost in a scene of appalling desolation, criss-crossed with a network of fine lines scarred by pools of stagnant water.[109]

10

THE GOTHA RAIDS

Suspension of the Zeppelin raids against Britain at the end of 1916 did not mean the end of German ambitions as far as bombing London was concerned. Long range bombers operating by day rather than by night, it was felt, might just be successful where the airships had failed.

The first daylight raid on London was actually made in 1916 by a single LVG two-seater but the machine was shot down by French anti-aircraft fire as it attempted to return to base and the photographs, taken by the observer, of London under attack were lost, along with their propaganda value.

As German-held territory was still, by the end of 1916, still too far away to allow easy flights towards London and the Home Counties, the first priority for the Germans was to develop aircraft with the range and capacity to hit the British homeland.

Numerous aeroplanes were tried. The original Gotha bomber actually first flew in 1915 but various developments in the machine were soon introduced and large scale production of the Gotha G-1V did not commence until the beginning of 1917. With this machine now available, an independent bombing force, the Kogenluft, was established and based at four airfields around the Gent area, some forty miles behind German lines. Hauptmann Ernst Brandenburg was appointed to take command of the so-called 'England Squadron'.[110]

The Gotha G-1V was a huge machine with a wing span of 78 feet, a fuselage of over 40 feet, and was powered by two massive 260-horse-power engines. Carrying a crew of three it was also equipped with the new Goertz bomb sight and three Parabellum machine guns. A pay load of seven 50-kg bombs and six 12.5-kg bombs was carried by this enormous aircraft which, to most on-lookers, could surely never get off the ground.

Once in the air, however, the Gothas were a formidable force. Crews had been trained at Freiburg and had undergone acclimatisation on seaplanes to get used to flying for long periods of time. They flew in a diamond formation, each plane offering protection to other aircraft and also maximising the effect when bombs were dropped. Quite apart from its offensive and defensive values, the formation, when viewed from below, looked terrifying.

Hauptmann Brandenburg, the fuselage of his Gotha painted bright red for recognition purposes, had no illusions. He knew that his bombing squadron

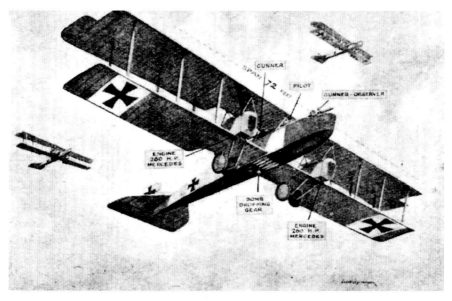

Giant Gotha bombers took over attacks on the British mainland in 1917. Huge aircraft, they flew in a diamond formation that, when viewed from below, seemed terrifying.

would be faced by heavy anti-aircraft fire and by a host of British fighters. Simply getting to the target would be difficult, getting home even worse. It was a risk that had to be taken.

By the middle of May 1917 the Gotha crews were ready and after formal inspections and visits from people like Field Marshal Hindenburg and General Hoeppner, the 'England Squadron' became operational.[111]

THE ATTACKS

The first serious and large-scale raid on Britain took place on 25 May 1917. Twenty-two bombers (one had turned back with engine trouble shortly after take-off) crossed the English coast where they managed to evade the dozens of planes – most of them obsolete old BE 2 machines – that had been scrambled to intercept them. Bad weather saved London that day as thick cloud closed in to shroud the city and, reluctantly, Brandenburg gave the signal to abort the mission.

The Gothas still had to get back, however. Cloud and confusion caused disruption to their formation and, strung out over a distance of five miles, they should have been easy targets for the fighters. It did not happen. Rather than go home with full bomb racks, bombs were soon dropping on the villages of Harvel and Luddestown and on the town of Ashford where eighteen-year-old Gladys Sparkes was killed, the very first victim of a Gotha raid.

Even if houses were not utterly
destroyed by a bomb blast, the effect
of shrapnel caused havoc, smashing
windows, pitting walls and, if anyone
was caught in the open, sometimes
cutting victims in half.

The bombers flew on, appearing above the Channel port of Folkestone.
Bombs were dropped on military camps at Shorncliffe and Cheriton where
Canadian troops were stationed and on the town itself. Folkestone was
devastated by the attack, houses and shops being destroyed and hundreds
injured. In all, over ninety people were killed during the raid. Brandenburg
might have been thwarted over London but he and his Squadron had certainly
achieved his desired effect over Ashford and Folkestone.[112]

The raid of 25 May was just the start. There was a national outcry and the
government was forced to bring home one of the new SE5 Squadrons from
France to bolster defences. To begin with, at least, it made little difference. The
air raids continued.

On 13 June a force of fourteen Gothas, their bomb loads lightened to give
them extra speed, attacked the East End of London. After dropping bombs
on Margate and its railway station – killing three people, including a twelve-
month-old baby – the giant planes soon appeared over the city. Roads and
railway lines into the docks were damaged, the German newspaper *Frankfurter
Zeitung* quoting the words of one airman in its report:

We proceeded coolly and calmly over the suburbs as we wanted to hit the
centre - - - We gave them plenty – blow after blow from bursting bombs
in the heart of England. The sight over central London was wonderfully
impressive.[113]

Vast amounts of damage – not to mention death and destruction – were caused to the East End but unfortunately the bombers next target was a school, Upper North Street School in Poplar. Just as the pupils and staff were preparing for lunch, a bomb fell through the roof and detonated inside the building. Eighteen children were either killed immediately or died from their wounds; dozens more were seriously injured.

In total, 160 people were killed in that single raid and the outcry over the killing of defenceless and innocent children was enormous. Anti-German sentiment grew to an extent not experienced since the early days of the war. Windows were broken and anyone with a German sounding name was liable to be beaten up. In Germany, however, Brandenburg and his pilots had become heroes. Brandenburg was awarded the Pour la Mérite, the medal being given to him by the Kaiser himself. The award probably marked the highlight of the German bombing offensive.

The defences of Britain were immediately strengthened and the London Air Defence Area was created to oversee things such as air-raid warnings, anti-aircraft fire and searchlights. When Ernst Brandenburg broke his leg in an accident, command of the 'England Squadron' passed to Captain Kleine. He was a far more reckless leader than Brandenburg and sent out his planes in all types of weather. This, combined with improved defences around London, saw a sudden increase in Gotha casualties and in September 1917 the giant aircraft switched to night attacks on the city.

Increasingly, Gothas were intercepted or damaged on their way to their targets, often by RNAS planes flying out of France and Belgium. And if they weren't caught on the way out, they were certainly attacked on the way home.

In the raid of 31 October, five bombers out of a force of twenty-two were shot down. Even on a successful raid such as the one on the night of 5/6 December, when London was subjected to particularly heavy aerial bombardment, five more bombers were destroyed. When, early in 1918, Kleine was killed leading an attack, not on London but on troops in the Ypres area, the end was clearly in sight.

The attacks continued throughout the early part of 1918 but on the night of 19/20 May British defences were able to account for at least six Gothas. It was the last Gotha attack on Britain. With events in France beginning to take a turn for the worse, the German High Command switched the Gothas to attacks on troops and the raids on London came to a sudden but definite end.

Fifty-seven Gotha crewmen lost their lives in the raids while only twenty-eight British pilots were reported killed or missing. However, 1,414 civilians were killed, a further 3,416 being wounded in what was, really, the start of modern warfare where everyone, civilian and servicemen alike, were in the front line.[114]

Musée de l'Armée
" Gotha ", Avion de bombardement

A captured Gotha is here put on display in the centre of Paris.

Behold the end of a raiding " Gotha,"
A prey to Kentish fire,
Our boys at the guns have finished the Huns
And lit their funeral pyre.

The Gotha bombers were slow moving and were increasingly intercepted either on their way to England or on their return from an attack but, to begin with, they spread as much terror and mayhem as the earlier Zeppelin raids.

THE ROYAL AIR FORCE IS BORN

When war had been declared in August 1914, nobody could have imagined the way aeroplanes would develop. A totally new style of warfare gradually emerged from the chaos of the Western Front and, in particular, from the fear engendered by the Zeppelin and Gotha attacks on London and other parts of Britain. The thought of death raining down from above was more than the public and the military minds could bear.

The Royal Flying Corps had already become a huge machine and a vitally important part of the war effort. By 1917, there was no way the war could be run without a vast and effective flying service.

The first Air Board had been created in May 1916, a second in February the following year. A week after the first Gotha raid on Britain an increase in the size of the Royal Flying Corps was recommended by the War Office. The RFC, it said, should be extended from 108 Squadrons to a massive 200, and, in addition, the RNAS should also be increased in size and strength. As a result of these recommendations, on 11 July 1917 the South African Lieutenant General Jan Smuts was given the task of leading a Cabinet Committee on Air Defence and Organisation.[115]

Smuts and his Committee did not sit for long. By 17 August they had reported back on both aspects, clearly stating that an independent air force, a third service in addition to the army and navy, should be created. This would be headed by a new Air Ministry and should bring together both the Royal Flying Corps and the Royal Naval Air Service. The report was accepted and the Air Ministry came into existence on 3 January 1918. Sir Hugh Trenchard was appointed Chief of Air Staff (he was replaced in France by Sir John Salmond) and set about bringing together the RFC and the RNAS, amalgamating them into the new Royal Air Force.

The RAF came into existence on 1 April 1918 but, with the German Spring offensive – Ludendorff's last bid for victory – having been launched a few days before, the momentous moment was hardly momentous for most pilots. Indeed, for pilots like Victor Yeates, as shown in his fictional account of the war, uniform and pay were more important than reorganisation and who was taking control of the service:

> During the day an official document about the Royal Air Force circulated. The new regime was to commence on the first of April, which seemed to Tom an appropriate date. Bulmer, Moss and Debenham already had the strange new uniform - - - but it appeared that the uniform was not to be compulsory for the present and khaki might still be worn on all occasions. The rates of pay were not changed, but instead of being paid in advance pay would be in arrear, which would have the immediate effect of cutting out a month's pay.[116]

A recruiting poster for the RAF. The poster is dated and the drawings are primitive but it probably had its desired effect on youngsters.

Members of the new RAF line up for review by the King, proudly shaping their ranks into the letters RAF on the hillside.

The reorganisation of the flying services had little immediate effect on front line pilots. There was still a war to be waged, still aerial battles to be fought and it barely mattered if you fought them as a member of the Royal Flying Corps or the Royal Air Force. Ranks may change, uniforms might or might not be altered, money might well be delayed but, at the end of the day, all of that had little effect on whether a man lived or died up in the air.

Even for people currently serving at home there seemed little enough to worry about. For men like Cecil Lewis it was, once again, the uniform that mattered:

> My memories of that year at Rochford are crowded. Something always seemed to be happening. It was while I was there that the RFC and the RNAS merged into the Royal Air Force, and we all preened ourselves in beautiful new blue uniforms.[117]

For most pilots, 1 April was just a day like any other. In so many of the diary entries of airmen there are comments about the war but the reorganisation of the service receives barely a mention. For someone like Roy Crowden the change might never have happened:

> Caught about ten Huns in a shell hole. Four got out and started to run. Killed three as they tried to get away – a bit of my own back for yesterday. Had

When the RAF was formed it took over all equipment and bases from the RFC and the RNAS. The RNAS had established a training establishment at Cranwell in April 1916 – naval personnel being held on the books of HMS *Daedalus* in the Medway. On 1 April 1918 RNAS Cranwell became RAF Cranwell. The base is still in use.

toothache all night. Feeling rotten so am staying in bed for the rest of the day. Have got two Huns down now. Cheers.[118]

The plan to create 200 operational Squadrons never quite came off. But by the time of the Armistice in November 1918 the RAF had 188 separate Squadrons with a total of 22,647 aircraft and 291,170 men. It was a major fighting force.[119]

THE INDEPENDENT AIR FORCE

One of the recommendations of the Smuts Committee report was that the war in the air had to remain an offensive war. As a result, in February 1918, VIII Brigade was formed to carry out independent bombing raids over Germany. The RNAS had been planning and operating night raids into Germany since October the previous year and the new Brigade included men and machines of both the RFC and the RNAS. In the first few months of 1918 the Brigade proceeded to launch several deep penetration raids into Germany.

These bombing raids quickly proved their worth. In fact, they were so successful that it was decided to expand the Brigade into the Independent Air Force. The name is confusing. By now the RFC and RNAS had been amalgamated into the RAF and the Independent Air Force, while operating independently of any of the Army Corps on the ground, was still an integral part of the RAF.

Sir Hugh Trenchard – always a man of firm convictions and beliefs – had found it difficult at first and, then, impossible to work with Lord Rothermere, the Secretary of State at the new Air Ministry. As a result, early in 1918 he had resigned, being replaced by Sir Frederick Sykes. That left Trenchard at something of a loose end and when the Independent Air Force was formed, he took command of what was, really, Britain's first bomber force on 5 June 1918.

As well as aircraft such as the DH9, DH4, FE2b – this last machine was now too old and obsolete to be used on anything other than night flying duties – and Sopwith Camels, the Independent Air Force was equipped with four Squadrons of Handley Page 0/100 and 0/400 heavy bombers.

The 0/100 had been built to Admiralty requirements from plans that had been drawn up as early as December 1914 and the 0/400 was a development of this earlier plane. The 0/100 first flew in 1915, the newer version a year later, coming into service in the spring of 1917. The original aim of the 0/400 was to mount retaliatory raids against Gotha bases but the coming of the Independent Air Force changed this role for ever.

The Handley Page 0/400 was a massive machine, having an upper wing span of 100 feet. With a length of 63 feet and powered by two Rolls-Royce Eagle

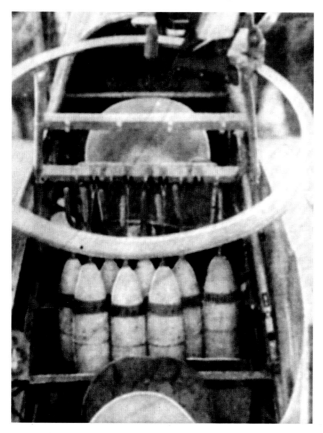

This photograph shows the bomb compartment in one of the many bombers used to attack Germany in the final year of the war.

2~Engine Handley Page — climbing.

A massive Handley Page bomber of the Independent Air Force lumbers into the sky.

engines it even dwarfed the massive Gotha. Carrying a crew of three and with
bomb stowage for sixteen 112-lb bombs, it was an aircraft to inspire awe:

> I climbed up the ladder into the front, then crawled through the tunnel into
> the cockpit. It didn't seem much different from those of the aircraft in which
> we flew at Stonehenge. The same two seats, for the pilot on the right and the
> observer on the left, the wheel on top of the control column for the pilot, the
> rudder pedals in front of it and the compass down on the floor to the right - -
> - We continued down to the river, whose banks were broad and sloping at this
> point, forming a wide valley. 'Very useful,' commented Harrison. 'Probably
> why they chose this field for o/400s. It enables you to get up speed a bit after
> take off before climbing.[120]

Many of the IAF bombing raids took place at night. There was no such thing
as radar and navigation was, at best, a chancy affair.

An early system of light beacons – lighthouses as they were called – were
set up to help guide pilots home, flashing lights that told aircraft exactly
where they were. It was all too easy to miss these lighthouses and, regardless
of defences such as searchlights, flaming onions and Archie, finding your way
home in the dark was one of the most dangerous things night bombers of the
IAF ever did.

Flare paths would be lit on the airfield, both for take-off and for landing. The
lights, usually oil or paraffin lamps, would be illuminated, but only for very

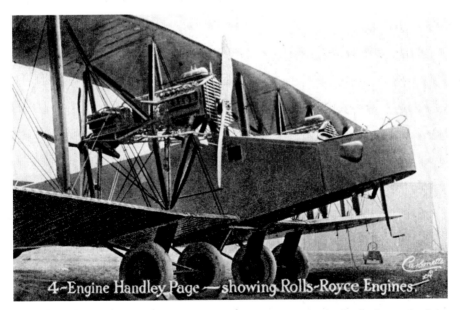

The four-engine Handley Page bomber that came into service in the final month of the
war. Its introduction had been delayed when the prototype crashed during trials.

brief periods as there was always a danger of enemy bombers being attracted by the lights. There were other dangers, too:

> The flight commander goes first, roaring down the lane between the flares and fading away into the darkness beyond. The other two follow at intervals of ten minutes. Richards, who is last to take off, creates some excitement by steering straight for one of the flares, knocks it over with his undercarriage, and leaves a miniature prairie fire behind him caused by the burning parrafin streaming over the dry grass.[121]

One of the advantages of night flying was that there were few enemy fighters to worry about and even anti-aircraft fire was less effective by night than it was by day. Searchlights were concerning, particularly when they caught a machine in their beams, but there was always one sure way of dealing with them:

> Richards throttles down his engine and dives swiftly towards the base of the beam. Just as the light catches him, his machine gun begins to stutter, and spurts a stream of bullets down the beam. The light goes out abruptly and the crew bolt for their lives - - - He smiles to himself and pulling the machine out of the dive, heads for another beam that has sprung up a short distance away. But as the hum of the engine is heard approaching, that also goes out without waiting to be fired on.[122]

The Independent Air Force continued to operate until the end of the war, dropping some 500 tons of bombs on German industrial plants such as engine factories and poison gas centres, railway junctions and iron foundries. It was a hugely successful enterprise and one that spawned the phrase that was later used in all accounts of offensive air tactics – the bomber will always get through.

A bomber from the Independent Air Force comes home after another raid on German industrial centres – a superbly evocative impression of night flying in the final years of the war.

11

GROUND SUPPORT

The concept of using aircraft for ground support was one of the main developments of the aerial war in 1917 and 1918. Of course lone operators – even groups of fighters – had swooped on trenches and shot them up, almost from the beginning of trench warfare. But before 1917 it had never been a coordinated and thought through tactic.

On 11 May 1917 all that changed when the RFC launched its first low-level attacks on enemy positions, low-level attacks that were coordinated with infantry assaults on the ground. Suddenly, air attacks were being made by waves of aircraft, usually operating beyond the range of the artillery barrage that accompanied any attack. Aircraft even remained above the battlefield to wipe out any enemy infantry left behind by the artillery and infantry. At least that was the theory.

In practice, German soldiers remained in their dugouts while the artillery barrage was raining down on empty trenches, then emerged, unscathed, to mow down the advancing British and French with machine gun fire. If any aircraft were still about they, too, were subject to fire from the machine guns which, at low level, were deadly accurate.

However, the British air attacks were successful enough for the Germans to quickly copy them. They even designated some of their Squadrons purely for ground support and equipped them with aircraft suitably reinforced with armoured plating. Such tactics certainly worked during the Battle of Cambrai in November 1917 when a surprise aerial attack was instrumental in throwing back the British infantry and recovering much ground that had been lost to the new British tanks. The British, of course, had no intention of designing special aircraft for the task – at least, not in the short term – and it was invariably left to the Camel Squadrons to offer much of the ground support.

The Camels were well designed for ground support work. Superbly manoeuvrable in the hands of an experienced pilot, very few people – sometimes not even the pilot – knew what the Camel would do next. They could dip and dart, turn on a sixpence – qualities that made them ideal for ground strafing. The trouble was, the pilots hated it:

A crashed German two-seater is inspected by British soldiers during the Battle of Cambrai.

The AEG was a German bomber introduced in 1916 with the main spars in the wings and their compression members made out of steel tubing. An armoured version of the plane (the J1) was intended for ground strafing. Armour plating made the aircraft virtually immune to ground fire.

Found some Huns at the edge of a wood. Got them. Blast this ground strafing. We lost too many people at it before - - - I'm damned hungry. Just can't get anything to eat.[123]

Pilots felt themselves to be particularly vulnerable when working close to the ground. Enemy aircraft and even Archie were occupational hazards that people faced, day in, day out. They knew that when an Albatross or Fokker Triplane dived at them it was a relatively fair contest; and anti-aircraft fire was really just a matter of good or bad luck, Archie would either hit you or he wouldn't and, somehow, the great masses of black smoke that accompanied his brief moments of anger and hate were expected.

But low down, perhaps just two or three hundred feet above the earth? That was an entirely different matter. Then skill and judgement mattered very little and no matter how good you were, luck invariably played a part in whether you lived or died. By the late summer of 1918 most pilots knew that both von Richthofen and Micky Mannock had been killed by machine gun fire from the ground. It was a worrying thought – if those two aces could be caught out in that way, what hope was there for the ordinary man? As Victor Yeates said:

According to the verbiage of brigadiers and colonels the Camel squadrons would be expected to stop the German advance by ground strafing: a gloomy prospect - - - The chance of surviving continuous low work for, say, a fortnight was not great. To do so meant being missed by several million machine gun bullets aimed particularly and personally at one.[124]

FLYING HIGH

If ground strafing caused pilots much concern so, too, did high altitude flights. Aircraft like the Sopwith Camel had a maximum ceiling of around 22,000 feet – although it was particularly ineffective at such altitude – while the SE5 and Bristol Fighter were more than efficient at heights of around 20,000 feet. The problem was not the machines, it was the pilots.

Nobody was trained in high altitude flying and they were certainly not equipped for it. Cockpits were open to the elements and gloves, flying helmets and overalls, which might well be effective lower down, were not really capable of helping pilots withstand the intense cold at high altitude. Even experienced and capable pilots like Jimmy McCudden found high flying a strain. After one patrol where he had taken his SE5 up to 21,000 feet, chasing a German Rumpler, he wrote:

I felt very ill indeed. This was not because of the height or the rapidity of my descent but simply because of the intense cold which I experienced up high.

A German aerial photograph showing British tanks moving into position ready for attack.

SE5 fighters flying low over the battlefield – normally low flying duties were left to the ubiquitous Sopwith Camels.

The result was that when I got down to a lower altitude, and could breathe more oxygen, my heart began to beat more strongly and tried to force my sluggish and cold blood around my veins too quickly. The effect of this was to give me a feeling of faintness and exhaustion that can only be appreciated by those who have experienced it. My word, I did feel ill, and when I got on the ground and the blood returned to my veins, I can only describe the feeling as agony.[125]

The German Rumplers were designed to fly high where the only Allied machine capable of catching them were the Sopwith Dolphins, introduced onto the Western Front in January 1918. Having a ceiling of nearly 22,000 feet, the Dolphins patrolled the upper regions over the lines and, wherever possible, other pilots were happy to let them go.

It was not always possible, of course, and the accepted tactic of 'waiting in the sun' meant that, all too often, prowling scouts were forced higher and higher to find their victims. The famous 'Hun getters' like McCudden knew the effects of high altitude flying and were more than happy to endure the discomfort if it brought them more victories. Other pilots were not nearly so happy with the technique:

We went fairly high, 17000 feet, and am feeling bloody in consequence. I don't think I can go on much longer - - - I simply can't stick any more high stuff.[126]

Without oxygen, without acclimatisation, it was a wonder more pilots did not succumb to the effects of high altitude flying.

OUT OF THE LINE

Pilots of the RFC and RAF – and of the French and German air services – might not have to endure the filth and horror of the trenches and they could, at least, wander off to the local estaminet each evening or enjoy a rowdy night in the Mess. But unlike front line soldiers their war was constant. Soldiers tended to spend a week or ten days in the trenches, and then have time out on rest. For pilots this was not normally possible. There was always a demand for their services and the daily patrols, the Dawn and Evening Patrols in particular, had to go ahead unless the weather was so bad as to prevent all types of flying.

The best that most pilots could hope for was a fortnight's leave every so often and, if they survived that long, a transfer to Home Establishment after six months at the Front.

Only very occasionally were Squadrons pulled out and sent back to places like St Omer, the main base for the RFC and, from 1914, the hub from which

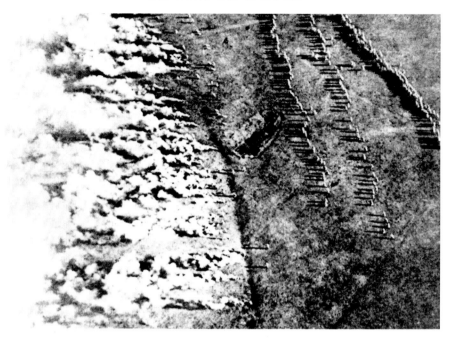

A photograph showing a gas attack on the Western Front. Pilots undoubtedly felt happy to be out of such combat – no matter how low or high they flew.

THE SOPWITH TRIPLANE

The Sopwith Triplane, flown mainly by squadrons of the RNAS. Pilots and Archie gunners often mistook it for the German Fokker Triplane – and vica versa.

all other aerodromes and Squadrons radiated. This usually occurred if they had suffered particularly heavy casualties and needed to induct a large number of replacements. Sometimes it happened when a Squadron was being re-equipped with different aircraft.

Whatever the reason, the rest period was always gratefully appreciated. St Omer was also one of the first places a new pilot might go to await his posting to a Squadron. It quickly became a sanctuary for pilots, a place of bars and restaurants and ladies of easy virtue. On 5 April 1918 Camel pilot Roy Crowden was moved to write in his diary:

> I am 19 today and what a present. We are going into rest for three weeks to get the Squadron together again and then I am going on leave. Cheers![127]

A few weeks later, having returned from leave and rejoined his Squadron in the St Omer region, he was writing about the rest period with undiminished joy:

> My hat, we've been resting now for over three weeks, having a glorious time. Dances given by lady ambulance drivers. Two topping girls, called Margery and Toni. Rather keen on Margery - - - Also topping bathing, either in the sea or a top hole pol. Plenty of dinner parties at the Continental in Calais. The only blot on the whole thing is the new Flight Commander, the finest 'shit' I have ever yet met.[128]

Rest periods, of course, were short lived and always there was the thought that, before too long, the war would begin again.

A FALL OF ACES

If the twelve months between the summers of 1916 and 1917 could be called the year of the aces, then the corresponding period between August 1917 and August 1918 was the year when so many of them were finally awarded Guynemer's 'wooden cross'. It was inevitable that, sooner or later, death would catch up with them, no matter how capable they might be as pilots and air fighters. The simple law of logic declared that the longer they carried on flying and fighting, the sooner they would be brought down and killed.

By the beginning of 1918 it was perhaps inevitable that von Richthofen's charmed life was coming to a close. He had been shot down by a British two-seater on 6 July 1917 but had survived the crash, albeit with severe head injuries. Never one of the most personable of men, he seemed to retreat into himself even more after the injury, as if finally realising that he was not immortal and that it would take only the faintest piece of bad luck to bring his glittering career to a conclusion.

BROUGHT DOWN IN FLAMES

An aerial combat high above Flanders.

On Sunday 21 April 1918 Richthofen and the members of his Flying Circus, as the British called them, were preparing to take-off. Much to the chagrin of the Jasta pilots, a mechanic stopped Richthofen and asked if he could take a photograph of the Red Baron. Boelcke had had his photo taken just before his final flight and since then the superstition had grown amongst German pilots – never have your photograph taken before going into combat. Richthofen had no time for such nonsense. He happily posed for the mechanic, then climbed into the cockpit of his Fokker Triplane and took off.

Already in the air and on course to meet the Circus was the combined might of No. 209 Squadron. Included in the mass of Sopwith Camels were Flight Commander Roy Brown, a twenty-four-year-old Canadian who, after over twelve months of continual air fighting, was nervous, exhausted and close to the limit, and newcomer Wilfred May, a fellow Canadian. Brown's instructions to May were to stay clear of trouble but no sooner had the two formations met than May found himself isolated and pursued by a blood-red Triplane.

No matter what he did, May could not shake off the German. Lower and lower they went, until it seemed that the end must come shortly. But Brown had seen what was happening and dived after the red Triplane. As he opened fire the plane was seen to stagger, its nose rose and then it glided easily and steadily to earth on the British side of the lines. When the members of the Australian 53rd Field Battery rushed to the plane they found the dead body of Manfred von Richthofen sitting silently in the cockpit.

Credit for bringing down the Red Baron was immediately given to Roy Brown, an understandable claim given the significance of the event. Brown himself believed that he had hit the plane but debate has always raged over who actually brought down Germany's greatest ace. Richthofen was killed by just one machine gun bullet and the angle of penetration seems, now, to indicate that the round was fired not from the air but from the ground. No autopsy was ever performed and Richthofen was buried the day after his death.

The duel took place at such low altitude that the red Triplane was fired on by more than one machine gunner from the ground. Certainly several of them claimed to have hit the machine. At this distance in time it is almost impossible to make firm decisions but, in all probability, one of them, rather than Roy Brown, fired the fatal shot. Manfred von Richthofen, the supreme aerial killer of the war, was almost certainly brought down and killed by ground fire.

Britain's highest scoring ace, Micky Mannock, did not survive von Richthofen for long. Always keen to help tyro pilots, on the morning of 26 July 1918 he took up Donald Inglis, a young New Zealander who had recently joined 85 Squadron. Mannock was intending to blood Inglis, to find an easy target and give him his first kill.

At about 5.30 a.m. they spotted a German two-seater above Merville. The enemy plane was soon falling to ground and, surprisingly, Mannock decided to follow the plane down, presumably to see if it had really crashed. Donald Inglis later wrote:

Falling in behind Mick again we did a couple of circles round the burning wreck and then made for home. I saw Mick start to kick his rudder and realised we were fairly low; then I saw a flame come out of the side of his machine; it grew bigger and bigger. Mick was no longer kicking his rudder, his nose dropped slightly and he went into a slow right-hand turn round, about twice, and hit the ground in a burst of flame.[129]

Mannock's SE5 came down just outside the German trenches. His body was buried where it fell but the grave, shelled and fought over several times since his death, has never been discovered. Whether he died in the flames – a death he feared more and more each day – or whether he had the chance to use the pistol he always carried with him will never be known.

James McCudden had already made his date with destiny. Just a few weeks before Mannock's death, flying to France to take command of his new Squadron, he ran into hazy weather over Auxi-le-Chateau and landed to ask directions. On taking off again, his engine was heard to cough and splutter. McCudden tried to turn back to the aerodrome – something he and other experienced pilots had always said should never be done at such a low height – and his SE5 nose-dived into the trees.

McCudden was found, thrown clear of the crash, bleeding from the nose and mouth but still alive. He was taken to the nearest casualty clearing station where he was diagnosed with a fractured skull. He never recovered consciousness. Later investigations revealed that, due to a design fault, a near vertical turn such as McCudden had employed on take-off would have flooded the carburettor of the SE5 and the machine would have lost power. In his last moments McCudden switched off the engine to reduce the risk of fire and undid his safety belt, presumably so that he could get out of the aircraft as soon as possible when it finally came to earth. Whether or not he would have survived had he stayed in the machine will never be known.[130]

Two of the most charismatic aces, Albert Ball and Georges Guynemer, died in 1917. When Albert Ball failed to return on 7 May, the German press was quick to announce that he had been shot down by von Richthofen. A few days later they rescinded the statement and gave credit to Richthofen's younger brother Lothar. Only after the war, when von Richthofen's account of his wartime experiences was published, did it become clear that on 7 May, when they were supposed to be fighting the pilots of No 56 Squadron, Manfred was on leave and Lothar was in hospital recovering from wounds. Ball's body, when found, had no marks on it and it was eventually decided that his death was either from engine failure or from Archie fire. Either way, his end is not clear.

Georges Guynemer was killed on 11 September 1917. He was seen to attack and destroy an enemy two-seater but was then set on by four German fighters and his companion, Lt Bozon Verduraz, lost touch with him. The wreckage of Guynemer's plane and his body were never discovered although the Germans soon claimed that he had been shot down by Kurt Weisseman. The German ace was himself shot down and killed two weeks later, by French pilot René Fonck.

Werner Voss was, in the eyes of many, a pilot to rival von Richthofen with forty-eight victories to his credit. He was mercurial and egotistical, a man who loved to drive fast motorbikes and usually took to the air without flying helmet or gloves. His final fight has gone down in legend.

On 23 September 1917 he was flying alone when he ran into seven SE5s from No. 56 Squadron. The British pilots were all recognised aces and included

Fighter pilots – one who survived and one who didn't. Charles Nungesser (left) survived the war only to die in an attempt to fly the Atlantic in the early 1920s. Georges Guynemer (right) was killed on 11 September 1917, shot down by Kurt Weisseman.

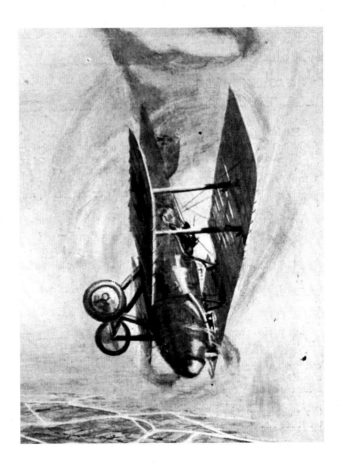

An Albatross D1 spinning out of control.

Jimmy McCudden, Richard Mayberry, Reginald Hoidge and Arthur Rhys-Davids in their number. Rather than try to escape, Voss decided to stay and fight. He was soon surrounded by the SEs but, such was his skill that he put bullets into every British machine, including the great McCudden's, and kept them at bay for over ten minutes.

Eventually, a burst of fire from Hoidge wounded the German pilot. Still he did not think of escape and the fight only ended when Rhys-Davids managed to get below him and empty a drum of ammunition into the Fokker. Voss went into a steep dive and crashed in a thousand fragments. As McCudden later wrote:

> As long as I live I shall never forget my admiration for that German pilot - - - His flying was wonderful, his courage magnificent and in my opinion he is the bravest German airman whom it has been my privilege to see fight - - - Rhys-Davids came in for a shower of congratulations and no one deserved them better but as the boy himself said to me 'Oh, if only I could have brought him down alive,' and his remark was in agreement with my own thoughts.[131]

Arthur Rhys-Davids, old Etonian and a man bound for Oxford once the war ended, was himself killed on 23 October. Leading the Flight in place of McCudden (who was on leave) he was last seen charging after a group of enemy machines. His death remains something of a mystery but is probably in keeping with his character.

There were survivors, of course. Udet and Goering both lived to play a part in the next war, as did men like Duncan Grinell-Milne, Billy Bishop and René Fonck. For many, however, Raoul Lufbery's pertinent comment held only too true, 'There won't be any after the war for a fighter pilot'.

OTHER NATIONS TOO

Austria-Hungary, Germany's main ally, played only a very limited role in the aerial war. Troops and flyers were quickly over-stretched and as the aerial might of Italy, their main opponent, began to grow the shortcomings of the Austrian air service were soon seen. However, despite a severe shortage of fighters, Hauptmann Godwin Brumowski did manage to shoot down forty enemy aircraft, no mean achievement on the Italian Front where the high mountains caused serious problems for aircraft.

By the time of the Armistice in November 1918 Italy had steadily increased its air force to over 6,000 aircraft. A total of 763 enemy aircraft, most of them Austro-Hungarian, had been destroyed.[132] The leading Italian ace was Francesco Baracca, although by far the most famous Italian airman was the fifty-one-year-old poet Gabriele d'Annunzio. After taking part in a seaplane

The Austro-Hungarian air service was largely ineffective throughout the war. This view shows a German built Aviatik-Osterreich, with pilot and mechanics, in the last few months of the war.

When they entered the war in 1917, America had no aeroplanes capable of combat flying and her air service was, therefore, forced to use the French SPAD as their main aircraft. America did, however, have a number of highly efficient and effective training machines, notably the Curtiss Jenny trainer, shown here at North Island, San Diego.

raid on Trieste in 1915, the Austrian government actually put a price of 20,000 crowns on the poet's head!

Although Russia had a number of flying schools in operation even before war began, the curriculum and course content that would-be pilots endured were exceptionally limited. And although Russia had a huge fleet of aircraft available, very few of them were of any use in war. Things did not improve much over the next three years, with the result that the air forces of Russia played little or no part in the war. Casualty rates of around 30 per cent were mainly due to crashes and accidents rather than enemy action.

America came late to the war although, as we have seen, American airmen had been serving with the French Foreign Legion for some time. When the USA did finally enter the war the immediate problem was aircraft. There were no American aeroplanes capable of taking part in the fighting – although the Curtis Jenny did prove a more than able training machine – and American pilots were forced to accept British and French aircraft.

In particular, the French SPAD was well used by American forces, some 4,000 of them being in service with the American Air Service before the war ended. When the American offensive in the St Mihiel area began in the autumn of 1918, General Billy Mitchell could call on 1,500 aircraft – British, French and American – to offer effective ground support with the result that huge gains were made. When the Armistice was signed there were forty-five American Squadrons in France – and the number was growing.[133]

12

THE WAR GOES ON

The Ludendorff Offensive, in reality three great drives by the German Army, began on 21 March 1918. It was a last throw of the dice by the Germans as, with American supplies, men and weapons arriving in ever growing numbers and with the Allied naval blockade beginning to strangle the morale of the German people, it was clear that if there was to be any hope of a German victory something would have to be done sooner rather than later.

With only a brief preliminary bombardment and launched over a countryside shrouded in thick mist, Ludendorff's initial attack took the Allies totally by surprise. Gas shells added to the confusion and when the German storm troopers – shock troops who moved quickly across the battlefield – arrived in the supposed location of the British and French trenches they found that many of them had simply been obliterated. The Allies plunged into a headlong retreat, sustaining 200,000 casualties.

For many British airmen, the German attacks meant yet another round of ground strafing as they tried to stem the rapid assaults. It was not a pleasant task but there was always the chance that enemy aircraft might venture too close:

> Misty in the morning, Hun pushing like Hell, absolute chaos behind our lines. Went off at midday to strafe troops and drop bombs on them. Got my first Hun. Caught him this side of the lines. Stock dived first and got the observer and I dived next, firing like blazes, and he started to go down in flames.[134]

For the first few weeks it seemed as if nothing could stop the German juggernaut. Initial gains were deceptive, however, and by late spring the German offensive had ground to a halt. More than anything, it was the shock of seeing the amount and quality of Allied equipment and weapons that caused the German troops to stop and wonder if they could ever succeed in their task.

Then came the Allied counter attack. It was a hard, grinding assault and slowly but surely the German armies were pushed back. It was clear, even by late summer of 1918, that Germany could not now win the war. It did not stop them fighting on, particularly in the air.

Handley-Page & Nieuport.

62.

Little and large – a giant Handley Page bomber and a Belgian Nieuport stand side by side on the airfield.

The Germans were severely hindered by a lack of fuel for their aircraft. From August onwards the Jagdstaffeln were allowed only 150 litres of petrol per aeroplane per day and with this basic allowance they had to fight a defensive war against the Royal Air Force that was growing steadily stronger.[135] Despite these crippling limitations, the three great Jagdstaffeln under Udet, Loerzer and Goering continued to battle hard against their opponents, desperately trying to stop the tide of Allied supremacy in the air.

In the closing months of the war, Anthony Fokker designed and built the Fokker D VIII, a monoplane with steel fuselage. It was Fokker's last involvement in the war effort and the new machine was quickly issued to the pilots of Richthofen's old Jasta. It was an aeroplane that might have made a significant difference to the aerial war but it came too late and, in the end, only thirty-six DVIII's ever served on the Western Front. Despite this, when, on 6 November 1918, three SPAD scouts were shot down, the DVIII became the last German plane to destroy Allied aircraft in the Great War.[136]

The dogfights continued almost to the end, both sides clearly intending to fight on until they were ordered to stop:

> Got set on by six Huns. My hat, they gave me a bloody time. They began on me at 700 feet. Huns don't like to get near the ground so I started to rev down, eventually hopping over trees about twenty feet up. Got one old Fritz just as he pulled up, preparatory to a dive on yours truly. Put a burst into him and down he went. It was confirmed later by 84 Squadron – a Phaltz Scout was seen to crash and mine was the only scrap that took place in that vicinity.[137]

THE ARMISTICE

The order to stop fighting came on 11 November 1918 although, with rumours of an impending Armistice circulating and consistently bad weather, there had been very little air activity for several days before that.

The initial reaction in most RAF Messes was one of wild rejoicing. It was time to throw a party without worrying about how you might feel on tomorrow's Dawn Patrol. It was only later that the reality of the situation really hit home. It was over, finally over, all the dogfights and the killing, all the Archie, all the ground strafing. The sense of relief was almost tangible. For some there was a feeling of missed opportunities:

> So it was over. I confess to a feeling of anti-climax, even to a momentary sense of regret. We were a new Squadron, fresh overseas, we wanted – particularly the new pilots – to justify our existence, to carry out in action the thing we had been trained for. Moreover, when you have been living a certain kind of life for four years, living as part of a single-minded and united effort, its sudden cessation leaves your roots in the air.[138]

For the French there was mainly sadness and relief. They had lost so many men, on the ground and in the air, and for some time now French pilots had been a little under par. Their aces, men like Fonck and Nungesser, were still chalking up their kills but the ordinary escadrille pilots left more than a little to be desired.

But the war was over. The Germans had been expelled from French territory and the 5,500 French airmen who had lost their lives during the war had clearly not died in vain. So, for the French Squadrons, it was time to raise a toast and silently remember their dead.

Escadrille No. 1 of the French Air Force. A pilot climbs into the cockpit of his SPAD. Escadrille No. 1, the Stork Squadron, was famous throughout France as the home of quality air fighters.

Germany had always made useful propaganda out of the exploits of her fighter aces. To the German public Richthofen, Udet and the others truly were 'knights of the air'.

German pilots sat despondently in their Mess Halls and barracks and wondered where it had all gone wrong. As far as they were concerned they had not been defeated and were more than willing to take to the air whenever the command was given.

The German Army Air Service had lost 6,840 airmen killed, 1,372 missing, and a further 7,350 wounded. In total, 3,128 aircraft had been lost along with twenty-six airships or Zeppelins.[139] Losses like that could not be taken lightly, especially when the war had ended in defeat.

It is, perhaps, easy to see why men like Goering and Udet began to harbour a grudge, feeling – knowing, as far as they were concerned – that they had been betrayed by the politicians and statesmen back in Berlin. With the Kaiser abdicated and in exile in Holland, it seemed as if their world had been turned upside down. There was worse to come.

Word soon arrived concerning the aircraft that were their pride and joy. And the news was devastating. Their aircraft were to be turned over to the victors, to the French and British air forces. As one member of Richthofen's Jasta later wrote, 'Im Krieg geboren, im Krieg gestorben – Born in the war – died in the war.' Many members of the German Army Air Service felt it was an appropriate epitaph.[140]

AFTERWARDS

In the wake of the Armistice, long before the Treaty of Versailles was signed, the German Air Service had been almost totally destroyed. A total of 2,000 fighters and bombers had been demanded by the Allies but as losses had been so heavy there simply were not this number of aircraft in the whole of the German Air Service and, as a consequence, the figure was reduced to 1,700. When these had been handed over, what aircraft were left returned to Germany with the armies and several of them were used in fighting that broke out against Estonia in 1919. However, by the terms of the Treaty of Versailles, the German Air Service was to be totally decommissioned and from 8 May 1920 it ceased to exist.

Peace also brought reductions in the air forces of both Britain and France. The war to end all wars had been fought and won; surely there was now no need of huge standing air forces? There was also the cost factor and by the time of Versailles the RAF had shrunk to just thirty-three squadrons. Britain had suffered huge casualty figures amongst its airmen – 6,166 killed, 3,212 missing or captured and 7,245 wounded – but with Hugh Trenchard once more appointed Chief of Air Staff it was clear that the mighty organisation that had grown up during the war years would remain in place and would, eventually, flourish.[141]

For the French, government policy soon dictated that for reasons national security, Germany must never be allowed to re-arm and assume a position of

The shape of things to come – the Vickers Vimy never saw service in the war but had the conflict gone on beyond November 1918 it would have become the main bomber used by the Independent Air Force.

Another aircraft that saw almost no war service, the Dupont HD3 was a two-seater French fighter that first flew in 1917 but did not enter service until October 1918. Although over 300 had been ordered the Armistice curtailed production and only seventy-five went on to serve with French Squadrons.

power in Europe. A powerful air force was part of the defence structure of the country, particularly a force of heavy bombers that could strike quickly and decisively into the heart of Germany.

So although, at the Armistice, France possessed over 3,000 aircraft, initially at least there was not the same wholesale destruction in the French Air Service as there was in Germany and, to a lesser extent, in Britain. There was a reduction, the number of escadrilles being cut back to just under 200, but the biggest mistake French aviation planners made was to fall behind other nations in the design of aircraft. By the mid-1930s the French Air Force was largely obsolete and it took the aerial campaigns of the Spanish Civil War to make them realise their mistakes. By then, of course, it was already too late.

AND THE MEN?

Demobilisation, for many, followed the end of the war. It was something men had been waiting for, hoping for, for years. Now, when it came, there was a major problem:

> [we were] baffled and, for the moment, disgruntled. But the readjustment was rapid and soon we began to explore the possibilities of peace. Where should we go? What should we do?[142]

For some, it was many months before they could return to civilian life. The Allies installed an army of occupation in Germany and aircraft were needed for this. Others, with definite jobs to go to – and with influence – were out of uniform far quicker than they could ever imagine. Cecil Lewis was one of these, back into civilian life within two months of the Armistice:

> Then the Squadron retired to its old aerodrome at Estree Blanche. As Senior Flight-Commander I was the first to get leave. A fortnight later I was in town. I went to Bertram Jones for advice as to what I should do. He sent me to General Caddell of the Vickers Aviation Department. Caddell took me on. Within another fortnight I was demobilized with a good civilian job: twenty years old.[143]

For some, like the German ace Rudolph Berthold, the violence of the war years simply would not go away. Always a fanatical nationalist, his political stance moved further and further to the right. Soon he had joined one of the many the anti-communist Freikorps formed to fight against 'the Reds' in the chaotic world of post-war Germany – the same hunting ground that spawned Adolf Hitler and the Nazi Party.

Berthold led and fought in many street battles where his ruthlessness was as apparent on the ground as it was in the air. He was killed on 15 March 1920 after a failed putsch, some saying that he was shot, others declaring that he was strangled with the ribbon of the Blue Max that he still habitually wore.

Flying had become a way of life for men like Lothar von Richthofen. Always a reckless pilot who probably spent more time in hospital recovering from injuries than most, after the war he became a commercial pilot. He ran mail and passengers between Berlin and Hamburg until, on 4 July 1922 his LVG machine crashed on what should have been a simple cross-country flight, killing him and most of his passengers.

Billy Bishop and fellow Canadian ace William Barker went into partnership in a private airline but the enterprise lasted only a few years before going bankrupt. Bishop moved to England to live, became an Honorary Marshal in the Canadian Air Force and eventually died peacefully in his sleep in 1953.

Eddie Rickenbacker, the racing driver, founded a motor company and an airline and lived an adventurous life to rival his wartime exploits. He survived two major aeroplane crashes, once drifting for twenty-four days in the Pacific before being rescued.

The career of Herman Goering is too well known to recount here. Suffice to say that, like many flyers, he found himself adrift and rudderless after the war. Always a fervent nationalist, he joined the Nazi Party and in due course rose to become commander of the Luftwaffe and Hitler's deputy. His involvement in the genocide of the 1940s ensured his trial as a war criminal but he managed to escape the hangman's rope by committing suicide a few hours before his execution. It was a far cry from the heady days of the Richthofen Jasta, but while his politics and character were undoubtedly reprehensible, there was no denying his courage.

Ernst Udet was probably the saddest of all the Great War aces. After finishing the war as commander of Jasta 11, Richthofen's old squadron, he, like Goering, joined the emerging Nazi Party. With his war record, he quite naturally became involved with the recreation of the German Air Force, rising to take control of the armament wing of the Air Ministry.

However, Udet's personal life was in turmoil and his always fragile personality soon came under immense strain. Never a friend or companion of Herman Goering, he did have to work with the Luftwaffe chief. Udet clashed with his chief on many occasions and after the Battle of Britain found that much of the blame for the defeat had been pushed his way by the ever manipulative Nazi Deputy.

Depressed and addicted to alcohol, early in 1941 Udet telephoned his mistress and, while she was talking to him on the phone, he shot himself. In a farewell message he blamed his mistress and the 'Iron Man' – Herman Goering – for his suicide. In keeping with the secretive nature of the Nazi regime, the

Lothar von Richthofen, younger brother of the Red Baron. He survived the war but spent several months of his service life in hospital because of reckless flying – otherwise his victory tally would have been considerably higher.

Two aces meet. Eddie Rickenbacker (left) shakes hands with Canadian Billy Bishop. Both men survived the war and went on to greater things.

Someone who certainly did not go on to greater things. Herman Goering sits in the cockpit of his Albatross, before the events of the 1920s and 1930s ensnared him and turned him into a member of the Nazi Party.

style of Udet's death was hushed up, authorities claiming that he had been killed while testing a new aeroplane.

For most of the airmen from the Great War peace meant simply the chance to pick up the pieces and start again. Some, like W. E. Johns, chose to stay in the RAF – at least until the opportunity to write and draw for a living presented itself. Others, like Victor Yeates, the author of *Winged Victory*, had to endure years of illness and suffering from TB – not unlike the fate awaiting Miller, one of the characters from his fine book.

Still others, like Roy Crowden, whose diary has been extensively quoted in this book, returned to their previous professions. In Crowden's case it was acting. Under the stage name of Roy Royston, he led an active and successful professional life, starring with famous names like Fred Emney, Arthur Askey and Richard Hearne (Mr Pastry). He even appeared in films, one of them, the 1966 *Plague of the Zombies*, becoming a cult classic.

For some, however, there could never be a going home. They were the men, on all sides, who had made the supreme sacrifice. Most are buried in military graveyards in France and Belgium, a few in cemeteries in Britain where their graves and memories are tended with loving care.

Still others – like Mick Mannock and Georges Guynemer – have no known grave. For them, a brief mention on the Thiepval and Menin Gate memorials are the only records of their passing – and their deeds of course, deeds that will live long in the minds and memories of anyone with a sense of history.

CONCLUSION

When war began in August 1914, aeroplanes were little more than pieces of wood held together by canvas and string. Anyone who even contemplated going up in one of them was considered half way to being certifiably mad. And yet, within the space of four short years the aeroplane had become one of the most potent military machines ever conceived by mankind.

In August 1914 one of the biggest fears was that the aircraft of the RFC would not be able to fly across the English Channel. By 1918 it was being done a dozen, two dozen, times a day. Long distance bombing raids were commonplace. And there were even experiments underway to enable aircraft to take-off from ships at sea with platforms being laid over the muzzles of guns.

An amazing weapon had been forged in the crucible of war, a weapon that would continue to develop and grow throughout the twentieth century. Perhaps it had not always been used in the most appropriate way but it was new, it was different, nobody had seen its like before. And so mistakes were bound to occur.

No matter how good or bad the aircraft were it was the pilots and observers – a remarkable breed of men – who made the aerial war a success or failure. And yet the young men who flew in the skies above France and Belgium would have been the very last to see themselves as heroes. They were, in their eyes, simply doing a job that needed to be done. To read their combat reports is to get in touch with their daily lives but there is nothing heroic or flamboyant in the way they are written. They are simply accounts of the actions as they saw them, an understated but vivid account of life in the air during the Great War:

> Whilst on reconnaissance over Cambrai my observer spotted a single EA diving down on one of our machines. He opened fire at a range of about 100 yards. After a short burst, EA fell in a slow spin and was seen to crash near a small clump of trees north of Cambrai.[144]

Those few, bland words contain and reflect a whole world of experience that most members of the RFC and RAF had never contemplated even four years before. Written by Lieutenant Benjamin Thomas, a twenty-four-year-old Welshman from Pembroke Dock, a man who was preparing to take up teaching as a career before the war gathered him up and propelled him into the skies over France, they are the words of someone who, like his comrades and opponents, was in the process of changing history – and he did not know it.

As far as flight was concerned, much more came out of the war than a weapon. Civil aviation, passenger and cargo planes, airports and airlines, dirigibles that could fly around the world – all of them owed their existence to those four years of confusion and mayhem between 1914 and 1918.

Truly, a monster had been spawned. The problem for mankind in the years ahead would be a simple one – how to control it!

NOTES/REFERENCES

1. Quentin Reynolds, *They Fought for the Sky*, pp. 115–116
2. Roy Crowden, 'Diary', 9 March 1918
3. Ibid, 20 July 1918
4. Peter Hart, *Aces Falling*, p. 342
5. Quentin Reynolds, pp. 29–30
6. Andrew P. Hyde, *The First Blitz*, pp. 3–4
7. Ibid, p. 4
8. Alex Imrie, *Pictorial History of the German Army Air Service*, p. 11
9. Joshua Levine, *Fighter Heroes of WW1*, p. 22
10. Alex Imrie, pp. 12–13
11. Ibid, p. 15
12. Chris Chant, *Air Forces of World War One and World War Two*, pp. 27–28
13. Joshua Levine, p. 22
14. Quentin Reynolds, pp. 34–35
15. Chris Chant, p. 62
16. Joshua Levine, p. 92
17. James McCudden, *Flying Fury*, p. 25
18. John Lloyd, *Aircraft of World War One*, pp. 15–20
19. James McCudden, p. 32 and p. 291
20. Quoted in Quentin Reynolds, *They Fought for the Sky*, p. 57
21. James McCudden, p. 41
22. Capt W. E. Johns, *Biggles, Pioneer Air Fighter*, p. 68
23. Quentin Reynolds, p. 63
24. Duncan Grinnell-Milne, *Wind in the Wires*, p. 45
25. Cecil Lewis, *Sagittarius Rising*, p. 35
26. Joshua Levine, p. 19
27. Quentin Reynolds, pp. 63–64
28. Ibid, pp. 66–67
29. Duncan Grinnell-Milne, pp. 25–26
30. Manfred von Richthofen, *My Life in the War*, p. 32
31. James McCudden, p. 46
32. Ibid, p. 46

33. Chris Chant, p. 51
34. Ibid, pp. 19–22
35. Manfred von Richthofen, p. 11
36. B. Thomas, Combat Report, 16 September 1918
37. Frank Owen, Letter, 15 January 1918
38. Ibid, 15 January 1918
39. Roy Crowden, 'Account of My Flying Experiences' (Paul Kemp Archive)
40. Roy Crowden, 'Diary', 20 July 1918
41. Corporal G. R. Butt, 'Diary', 2 September 1917
42. Frederick Oughton, *The Aces*, p. 13
43. Quentin Reynolds, p. 22
44. Quoted in Quentin Reynolds, *They Fought for the Sky*, p. 27
45. James McCudden, p. 88
46. Chris Chant, pp. 84–85
47. Ibid, p. 94
48. Alex Imrie, p. 33
49. Quentin Reynolds, pp. 131–132
50. Manfred von Richthofen, p. 63
51. Anon, 'With the Royal Flying Corps', article in *The Sphere*, p. 256
52. Ibid, p. 256
53. Joshua Levine, p. 136
54. Ibid, pp. 138–144
55. Alex Imrie, p. 21
56. Quoted in Quentin Reynolds, *They Fought for the Sky*, p. 151
57. Andrew P. Hyde, p. 36
58. Ibid, pp. 34–35
59. Frederick Oughton, pp. 120–122
60. Andrew P. Hyde, p. 36
61. Quentin Reynolds, p. 157
62. John Lloyd, p. 55
63. Ibid, p. 56
64. Ibid, p. 24
65. Martin Hale, *Fishguard's Great War Seaplanes*, p. 41
66. Ibid, p. 16
67. Billy Bishop, quoted in *The New York Times*, 3-2-1918
68. Roy Crowden, 'Diary', 5 June 1918
69. Alex Imrie, p. 34
70. James McCudden, p. 184
71. Conversation with Robert Turnbull Carradice, October 1964
72. Chris Chant, p. 57
73. John Lloyd, pp. 46–47
74. Ibid, p. 34 and p. 36

75. Corporal G. R. Butt, 'Diary', 22 August 1917
76. Ibid, 19 August 1917
77. Ibid, 11 October 1918
78. Capt W. E. Johns, *Introduction; Biggles, Pioneer Air Fighter*, p. VI
79. Roy Crowden, 'Diary', 19 February 1918
80. Ibid, 16 July 1918
81. Capt W. E. Johns, p. VII
82. Chris Chant, p. 56
83. Ibid, pp. 95–96
84. Victor Yeates, *Winged Victory*, p. 45
85. Quentin Reynolds, pp. 171–172
86. James McCudden, p. 182 and p. 183
87. Edward 'Mick' Mannock, quoted in *King of Air Fighters*, Ira Jones, p. 27
88. Chris Chant, p. 97
89. Quentin Reynolds, p. 133
90. Phil Carradice, *The Great War: An Illustrated History*, p. 113
91. Manfred von Richthofen, p. 66
92. Ibid, p. 64 and p. 76
93. Phil Carradice, *Alan Seeger: The American Rupert Brooke*, p. 32
94. Quentin Reynolds, p. 143
95. Ibid, p. 248
96. Quoted in *The Aces*, Frederick Oughton, p. 294
97. Interview with Robert Turnbull Carradice, October 1964
98. Roy Crowden, 'Diary', 4 June 1918
99. Ibid, 23 February 1918
100. Victor Yeates, p. 175
101. W. B. Yeats, *An Irish Airman Foresees His Death*
102. Jeffrey Day, *On the Wings of Morning*
103. Paul Brasher, quoted in *Voices of Silence*, p. 182
104. Capt French, quoted in *Voices of Silence*, p. 186
105. Meg Crane, article in *Siegfried's Journal*, winter 2011, p. 27
106. Anon, poem in *The BEF Times*, 1 November 1917
107. Victor Yeates, p. 162
108. Peter Beresford Ellis and Jennifer Schofield, *Biggles: The life of Capt WE Johns*, p. 135
109. Capt W. E. Johns, p. 69
110. Andrew P. Hyde, pp. 69–70
111. Ibid, pp. 69–71
112. Ibid, pp. 77–100
113. Ibid, p. 124
114. Ibid, pp. 180–181
115. Chris Chant, p. 56

116. Victor Yeates, pp. 130–131
117. Cecil Lewis, p. 165
118. Roy Crowden, 'Diary', 1 April 1918
119. Chris Chant, p. 57
120. Humphrey Wynn, *Darkness Shall Cover Me*, p. 3 and p. 7
121. Anon, Article in *The Sphere*, pp. 72–73
122. Ibid, p. 73
123. Roy Crowden, 'Diary', 15 July 1918
124. Victor Yeates, p. 44
125. James McCudden, pp. 269–270
126. Roy Crowden, 'Diary', 18 July 1918
127. Ibid, 5 April 1918
128. Ibid, 24 May 1918
129. Ira Jones, *King of Air Fighters*, p. 249
130. Peter Hart, p. 198
131. James McCudden, pp. 200–201
132. Chris Chant, p. 64
133. Ibid, p. 71
134. Roy Crowden, 'Diary', 22 March 1918
135. Alex Imrie, p.59
136. John Lloyd, p. 54
137. Roy Crowden, 'Diary', 31 March 1918
138. Cecil Lewis, p. 175
139. Alex Imrie, p. 60
140. Quentin Reynolds, pp. 270–271
141. Chris Chant, p. 59
142. Cecil Lewis, p. 175
143. Ibid, p. 175
144. Lt B. S. B. Thomas, Combat Report, 16 September 1918

BIBLIOGRAPHY

PRIMARY SOURCES

Newspapers and Magazines
The BEF (Wipers) Times
The Sphere
Siegfried's Journal
The New York Times
The Western Mail

Diaries/Letters
The Diary of Lt Roy Crowden (Paul Kemp Archive)
Letters of Corporal G. R. Butt (Paul Kemp Archive)
Letters of Sgt Frank Owen (Paul Kemp Archive)
Combat Reports of Lt Benjamin Thomas (Paul Kemp Archive)

Unpublished MS
'Account of My Flying Experiences, 54 Squadron RFC' (Paul Kemp Archive)
by Lt Roy Crowden

Interview
Robert Turnbull Carradice, October 1964 (copy held by author)

SECONDARY SOURCES

Phil Carradice, *The Great War: An Illustrated History* (Amberley, Stroud, 2010)
  Alan Seeger: The American Rupert Brooke (Cecil Woolf, London, 2011)
Chris Chant, *Airforces of World War One and World War Two* (Galley Press, London, 1979)
Peter Beresford Ellis & Jennifer Schofield, *Biggles: The Life of Capt WE Johns* (Veloce, Dorset, 1993)
Brian Gardner (Editor), *Up the Line to Death* (Methuen, London, 1964)
Duncan Grinnel-Milne, *Wind in the Wires* (Mayflower, London, 1968)

Martin Hale, *Fishguard's Great War Seaplanes* (Paterchurch Publications, Pembroke Dock, 2007)

Peter Hart, *Aces Falling* (Weidenfeld & Nicolson, London 2007)

Andrew P. Hyde, *The First Blitz* (Leo Cooper, Barnsley, 2002)

Alex Imrie, *Pictorial History of the German Army Air Service* (Ian Allan, London, 1971)

Capt W. E. Johns, *Biggles: Pioneer Air Fighter* (Thames, London, undated)

Ira Jones, *King of Air Fighters* (Greenhill Books, London, 1989)

Joshua Levine, *Fighter Heroes of WWi* (Collins, London, 2009)

Cecil Lewis, *Sagittarius Rising* (Corgi, London, 1969)

John Lloyd, *Aircraft of World War One* (Ian Allan, London, 1958)

Lyn Macdonald, *Voices and Images of the Great War* (Penguin, Lonon, 1991)

James McCudden, *Flying Fury* (Casemate, Newbury, 2009)

Vivien Noakes, *Voices of Silence* (Sutton, Stroud, 2006)

Frederick Oughton, *The Aces* (Consul Editions, London, 1962)

Quentin Reynolds, *They Fought for the Sky* (Pan, London, 1960)

Manfred von Richthofen, *My Life in the War* (Ace Books, New York, 1969)

Brenda Watts, *Belgrave Cemetery Roll of Honour* (Friends of Belgrave cemetery, Belgrave, 2008)

Humphrey Wynn, *Darkness Shall Cover Me* (Airlife Publishing, Shrewsbury, 1989)

Victor Yeates, *Winged Victory* (Cape, London, 1961)